DUBLIN
a city in crisis

0950462802

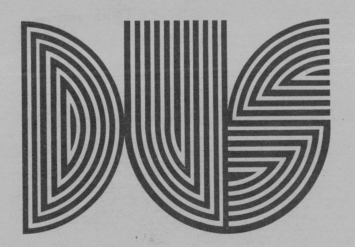

DUBLIN URBAN STUDY

Published by the Royal Institute of the Architects of Ireland.

Printed by Mount Salus Press Ltd., Dublin

Introduction

Dublin is a city in the process of renewal and expansion — a process inevitable in a situation where both the population and the economy are expanding. Because of the speed of development in the latter half of this century, both our architectural heritage and the human needs of our people are endangered.

Dublin shares this dilemma with most capitals and with many other great cities whose population or economy are expanding; but Dublin has the advantage of being able to see the results, both desirable and undesirable, of renewal and expansion in other cities, before the process of change has gone too far here.

Renewal and expansion need not be carried out at the expense of our architectural heritage or the human needs of our people.

Indeed, if carried out with sensitivity and concern, the re-creation of Dublin could enhance that existing heritage while ensuring that our temporary needs are met by buildings and spaces of high environmental quality. Awareness of the city's potential both as a repository of the past and as an expression of confidence in the future, is strong in many. Unfortunately, not all the citizens of Dublin have this awareness; and many who do lack the conviction or the will to ensure that the potential of Dublin is attained.

Dublin has an historic core with character and quality and a natural setting of incomparable beauty. Conviction and determination can save these qualities in Dublin.

Pressures of population; physical decay of the older fabric; hasty and piecemeal solutions; above all the virtually uncontrolled intrusion of the motor vehicle on the city and its environment, could combine to sap and to degrade the city structure. Yet as the following pages show few of the problems are without solution and, because of their scale, it is not too late to find solutions.

Solutions cannot be found without a clear identification of the major issues involved. This Dublin Urban Study has been prepared by the Royal Institute of the Architects of Ireland in an effort to identify the major issues as seen by the architectural profession, which is deeply concerned and conscious of the magnitude and difficulty of the task ahead. Study papers present the work of individuals or groups within the Institute; the opening and closing sections —namely, "The Faces of the City", and the "Summary and Conclusions", which contain firm recommendations for action — have been endorsed by the Council of the Institute.

I wish to thank those members of committees who have worked so hard to bring the Study to fruition and the sponsors who generously donated funds to finance its preparation and publication.

The Study is dedicated by the Council of the Institute to all the citizens of Dublin who can, by conviction and determination, influence the future growth and evolution of their city.

PADRAIG MURRAY, PRESIDENT RIAI

Editor's Preface

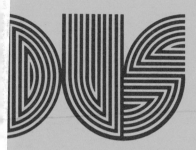

This Study was first begun in 1970 by the RIAI Planning Committee on the suggestion of three of its members, Hugh Brady, James Fehily and Brian Hogan, under the leadership of the then chairman Louis Adair Roche. The brief at that time was to examine the Dublin Urban Landscape and to recommend a comprehensive policy for its preservation and enhancement. Generous sponsorship was received from a number of firms and organisations towards research and preparation of material.

As the Study progressed, it became clear that wider issues had to be examined. The fabric of the city is woven from its buildings, streets, furniture and the spaces linking them; and while social and economic issues do not lie specifically within the professional expertise of the Institute, it was evident that these issues could not be ignored, since they vitally affect the quality of life of the people of Dublin. Existing social and community patterns — the way in which people's lives are expressed in and affected by the city's built form — could not be ignored.

Central to the problem is therefore that of Infill — the way in which new buildings are added to the existing fabric. All new city buildings are a form of infill, in that they must relate not only to their immediate neighbours but to the style and atmosphere of the city as a whole. This does not mean that contemporary buildings should automatically aim to copy past styles: it does mean, however, that designers of new buildings must observe general rules of good manners towards the existing fabric, particularly in regard to scale and texture, save where there are very good reasons to the contrary.

The Study was therefore broadened in scope so as to consider not only the original elements of open spaces, planting, street surfaces and street furniture but the wider issues which infilling raises. These included: the case for and against attempted reproduction of past historical styles; the form which new buildings should take in order to avoid disruption of the existing city pattern, where this was worthy of retention; the special role — positive or negative — of tall buildings; the scale and form of open space about, between and within buildings; and the potentially disruptive role of the motor vehicle — the way in which road planning, if considered in isolation, can disrupt not merely the physical appearance of the city but also the pattern of existing communities, which are the soul of the city and the main reason for its continued existence.

The issues are complex, the possible solutions manifold. The fourteen study papers — each contributed by members who have been concerned with particular aspects of urban design problems — do not always agree in detail as to how a specific problem should be solved. There emerges from the Study as a whole, however, an impressive degree of concensus on the urgent need to re-evaluate the total physical fabric of the city we have inherited, and to conserve in a realistic way the best of that heritage — identifying those characteristics and features which are important and which

make it different from other cities — rather than passively allowing it to decay through indifference, or actively sweeping it away in the name of supposed progress.

While the Study has been written entirely by members of the Institute, its preparation has been greatly aided by a number of contributions from outside bodies and individuals, and it is our pleasant duty to record our deep gratitude to all those who so freely gave of their time and dedicated scholarship, and whose views have been woven into the Study itself and particularly into its concluding recommendations for action. From the host of those who helped, especial thanks must go to Mr. Joe McCullough and Mr. Jim Mansfield for their penetrating analysis of the shortcomings of new suburban areas; to Dr. Maurice Craig for generous advice and encouragement; to Professor Kevin B. Nowlan for his pertinent comments on the conservation of worthy 18th and 19th century buildings; to Mrs. Maria Gaj and the late Mr. Maurice Gorham for their views on the advantages of living in a living city; to Councillor Ruadhri Quinn for his comments on the role of the elected representative in the planning process; and to Mr. Patrick Shaffrey of An Taisce for his emphasis on the necessity to subordinate traffic and transportation policy to real community need, rather than allowing the motor vehicle to absorb too much attention and capital investment, to the detriment of other more important values.

The Dublin Urban Study could not have been begun without the generous support of the original sponsors who funded the initial reserach work. To all these, who are listed overleaf, the committee extends its gratitude. Our warmest thanks above all must go to Allied Irish Banks Ltd. who have so kindly and generously sponsored the actual preparation and publication of this book.

Dublin, like so many other great historic cities, is in grave danger of losing its flavour and identity because of the demands and pressures of modern life. That flavour and that identity are so strong, so worthy of being kept, that all those who reserve them should be prepared to work for their conservation. This book provides not a mere forum for discussion, but a plan of action.

Some final words of thanks — to Seamus Ward and the Institute staff for patient and efficient back-up services; to Desmond Kinney and Ralph Dobson for their inventive skill; and to Mount Salus Press Ltd. for their technical dexterity in seeing through the presses this highly complex publication.

Reader, join us in our thanks to all these good people, but do not read only. Instead, seek to bring to reality some of the very practical dreams which are here set out.

Patrick M. Delany,
Editor.

Steering Committee

Chairman: Andrew Devane
            Hugh Brady
            James Fehily
            Peter Hanna
            Brian Hogan
            James Pike
Editor: Patrick Delany

Sponsors

Allied Irish Banks Ltd.
Cement Ltd.
G. & T. Crampton Ltd.
First National Building Society
Gouldings Horticulture Ltd.
Hardwicke Ltd.
Irish Life Assurance Co.
Irish Nursery & Landscape Co. Ltd.

Irish Permanent Building Society
Thomas McInerney & Co. Ltd.
New Ireland Assurance Co.
Hugh O'Neill & Co. Ltd
Roadstone Limited
John Sisk & Son (Dublin) Ltd.
Wates & Co. Ltd.

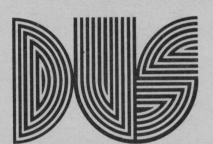

Illustrations and Acknowledgements
Back and front cover—photos by courtesy of Bord Failte
Malton prints pp. 5 and 6, Mitchell etching p. 7- photos
    by courtesy of National Gallery of Ireland
Photos p. 9, 1.12, 3.1, 3.2, 3.4, 7.7, 7.14, 12.11, courtesy Bord Failte
Drawing p. 15 reproduced from Dublin Advisory Regional Plan 1966
    with permission of the Controller, Stationery Office, Dublin
Map p. 24 and all other drawings based on Ordnance Survey maps
    by permission of the Government (permit no. 2440)
Photo 1.4—Rex Roberts Studios
Photos 2.2, 2.3—Lawrance Collection
Photos 3.3, 3.6—Colm O'Donovan
Unidentified photos by Deegan Photo, Barry Kinsella, Richard Daan

Photos 4.3, 4.5, 9.1—Bill Hastings
Drawing 6.3—Richard Dowling
Drawings A.23, 7.2, photos p. 7 and 7.16—from "The Antique
    Pavement" by Derry O'Connell by courtesy of An Taisce
Photos 9.9, 9.10, 10.6, 10.7, 10.10, 11.0, 11.01, 11.04, 11.06 and
    12.3—Piertse Davison International
Photos 11.3, 11.7, 11.9, 11.10—Henk Snoek
All drawings for paper no. 10 (pp. 74-80) by Deirdre O'Connor
All other photos by contributors, editor or anon.

Graphic Design by Kinney and Dobson

© Royal Institute of the Architects of Ireland, 1975

The Faces of Dublin

The Faces of Dublin

Our Inheritance

The city we have inherited is a product of history and of geography: a location shaped by wars and occupation and formed by builders and merchants. The site of the original settlement can still be identified and each succeeding age has left its imprint. While Dublin witnessed the same major events as the rest of the country, its participation was different. Like other cities, its position and surroundings influenced the timing, shape and type of development. In the course of time Dublin assumed its own identity. The character of the place is therefore not simply buildings or waterfront, but how these were laid out in a certain way, the materials chosen and the method of putting them together; the elements of nature contained in the man-made; the experience as one moves around. These are all aspects of the Urban Landscape and taken together give the city its personality.

The evolution of the city

A city is constantly changing, never static. Its major periods of growth or decline can be depicted in map form while acknowledging the fact that social or political factors may be the real cause for the amount of building or degree of stagnation. The emergence of Dublin is shown in the map sequence which follows, and the main factors contributing to development are then identified for each major area.

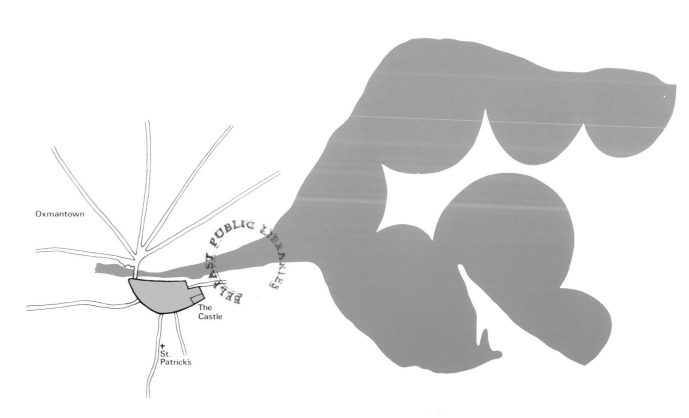

MAP A: Ford at the Hurdles — 800-1170

Little is known about the earliest Dublin. Baile Atha Cliath or the Ford of the Hurdles seems to have begun as a village settlement on the ridge of a hazel treed hilltop (along the line of the present High Street). At the foot of the hill ran the River Liffey crossed by a ford. Northwards were a series of roadways, the main one of which led to Tara of the Kings. With the coming of the Vikings, the village because of its river location assumed a new importance. They built a fortified village, used it as a port of call for their boats and gave it the name Dyflinn · Dubhlinne or dark river pool. Relations between the two communities was naturally hostile but in time their interests merged. A quay wall recently uncovered near Christchurch, house beams (on one of which a Viking ship is carved) on the hill slope and a timber lined road indicate the Norseman's site. As trade developed, stone walls were erected to protect the houses of timber or wattle and daub and for 300 years this was a Norse settlement even after the defeat at Clontarf. Converted to Christianity they built Christ Church in 1040.

MAP B: Stronghold of Conquest — 1170-1610

*Within a year of their landing in 1169 the Normans captured Dublin
and so began its role as a centre of conquest, a stronghold for
Anglo Norman and English settlers. A municipal town charter was
granted in 1172 thus establishing the administrative framework
—mayor, freeman etc.—still used. Colonists arrived from Bristol,
some Norse remained, others resettled outside the walls, the first
suburbia was established: Villa Ostmanoruim ('the town of the
easterners') at Oxmantown north of the Liffey was established.
Throughout the Medieval period of warfare, confiscations and
plantations in the country, Dublin became focal point of the pale.
Its massive stone walls and fortified gates guarded the maze of
narrow dark streets with their wooden or timber framed houses on
narrow sites faced with mud and rubble held together by laths and
ties. The more prosperous had stone build houses. Rural
depopulation and other factors led to the growth of an 'Irishtown'
outside the walls, a ghetto-type concentration of mud huts—mainly
on the south side—often with its own laws, customs, parish church
(St. Patrick's) and identity. North of the river most of the land
belonged to the monks of St. Mary's Abbey. As commercial activity
improved, the city experienced urban renewal within its walls and
more orderly suburban growth outside. The earliest printed map of
Dublin was made by John Speed in 1611, a city no more than
½ mile wide between east and west gates.*

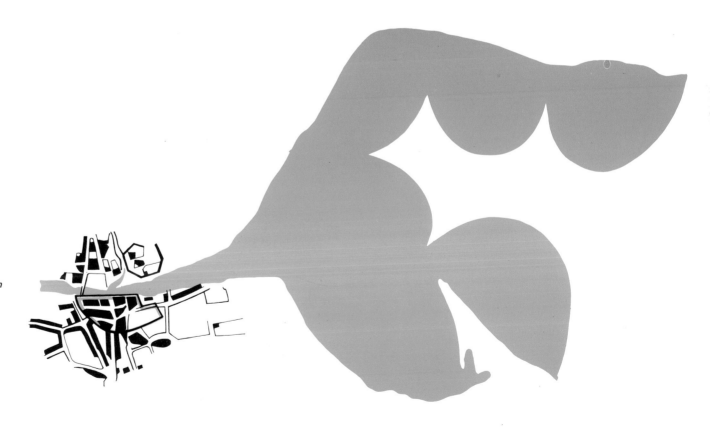

MAP C: From Alleyways to Squares — 1610-1685

With the collapse of the Gaelic Resurgence, Ireland became increasingly dominated by England and events there. Social and economic impacts were felt but very often the effects were different in Dublin to the rest of the country. Much of the commercial activity between the two countries went through Dublin and its port. Land in the harbour area was reclaimed and quay walls extended to deal with flourishing business. A building boom resulted in the city dismantling its old walls, expanding into the surrounding countryside and developing on a more regular pattern— the winding medieval streets of the old city gave way to streets and squares northward along Capel Street and the new bridges, westwards to Cornmarket and eastwards to Dame Street. The Phoenix Park was made available to the citizens (1662) and what was once an unenclosed common was laid out as St. Stephen's Green (1664-5). During this period of rapid expansion the city tripled its population to 64,000 persons.

4

MAP D: The Eighteenth Century —1685-1783

The eighteenth century saw the evolution of the city into the form which we recognise today. The familiar three to four storey residential blocks built of brick coming in as ships ballast—their plain pattern offset by ornate doorways, stone steps, iron railings and balconies while inside foreign and native plasterworkers and craftsmen decorated ceilings, walls and fireplaces. A start was made on many of the important public and private buildings which still provide focal points—The Parliament House (1729 onwards), Trinity College (1759), The Royal Exchange (now City Hall—1769), The Blue Coat School (1773) as well as theatres, clubs, town houses, many of which have long since vanished. The wide street commissioners began their activities improving the narrow and dangerous streets and creating broad new regular thoroughfares and paved footpaths. The Grand Canal system began and its terminus was sited just west of the city at St. James parish. During this century the city doubled its population to about 170,000 persons.

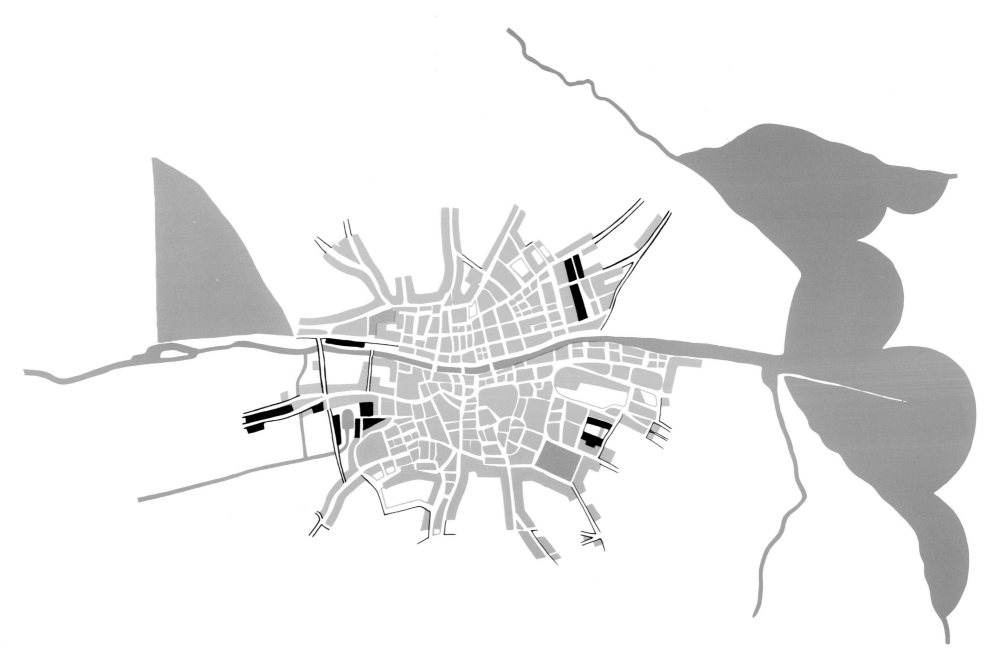

5

Artistic city planning and design reached its fullest expression in Georgian Dublin, seat of an assertive Parliament and capital of an impoverished colony deserving of the comment 'there never was so splendid a metropolis for so poor a country'. Elegant squares and gardens embellished the pleasantly proportioned streets as more superbly fashioned public buildings were completed: The Custom House (1791), The Four Courts (1803), The G.P.O. (1818), The Kings Inns (1816). As a result of these activities the direction and centre of gravity of the city shifted from an east-west to a north-south axis along Sackville Street, Carlisle Bridge (1793), Westmoreland Street and thence to College Green. Fashionable districts were created by major landowner developers on the south side (Fitzwilliam) and on the Northside (Gardiner) extending as far as the circular roads. Dublin was thus confined to an oval about 2½ miles long by 2¼ miles broad. Immediately outside the canals were completed—Grand to the South, Royal to the North—to connect waterways and harbour. Following the Act of Union, the city suffered a setback, and many of its patrons left. With unfavourable trading laws prosperity declined and with it, building activity.

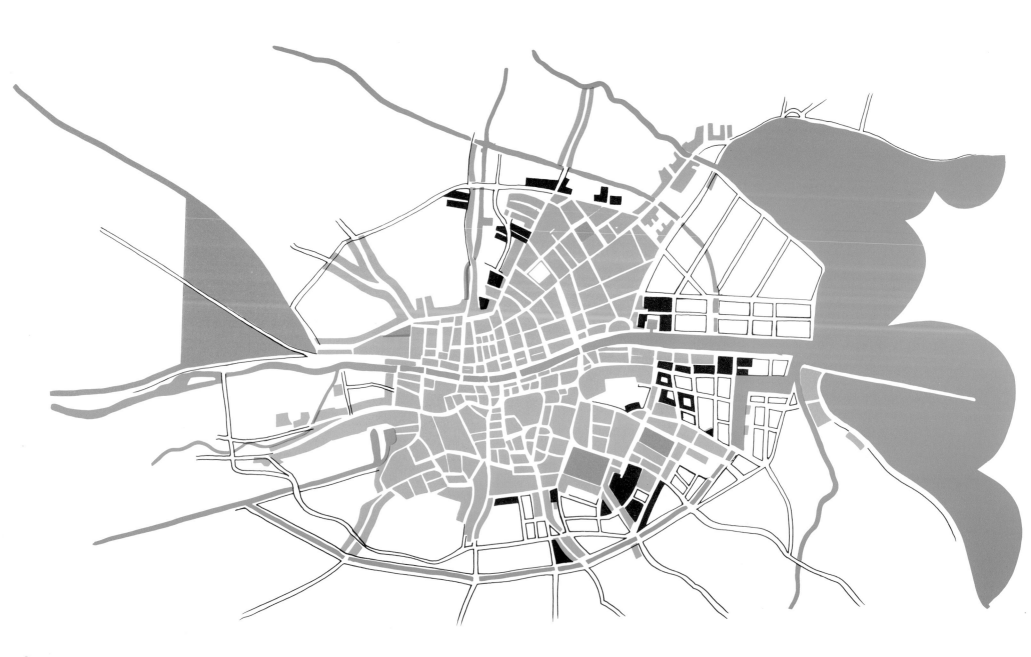

The 19th Century was an anticlimax for the city marked by the famines of the 20's and the 40's, by the exodus of the wealthy to the city fringe at Donnybrook, Ranelagh and North Strand and the influx of the poor into the central sectors of the city. Engineering skills brought into being the Bull Wall and the five railway stations from which the national railway network radiated and finally tramways made their appearance. As Dublin expanded, mainly to south and east, the house style changed to a two-storey over basement for the middle classes—Wellington road a beautiful example—and a two storey or one outside two inside for more modest means as seen in Heytesbury street area and in Phibsboro. Dun Laoghaire, Dalkey and Killiney now reached by public transport became fashionable residential areas and daytrip resorts, especially along the new pier and promenade. As the century closed the city population numbered about 350,000 persons.

MAP G: Recovery and Stability — 1897-1958

By far the most serious aspect of Dublin life was the appalling extent of squalour in the crowded tenements, which as late as 1938 averaged 18 per persons per dwelling unit in the central area: Decay and obsolescence in the older parts of the city, disused canals, new cramped housing areas at Ringsend and Fairview happening at a time of new nationhood—the task of slum clearance and new expansion slowly gained momemtum and new districts emerged—Cabra, Inchicore, Drimnagh, Marino, Clontarf, Donneycarney, Ballyfermot. With more widespread car ownership and improved economic conditions development began to scatter in ever widening circles even as the trams were replaced, bicycles became less numerous and the city finally emerged from its wartime austerity. But the anxiety to provide housing quickly and cheaply led to an achievement somewhat marred by the fact that one class districts were created, often dreary and monotonous, lacking in character and identity. There were by now 650,000 living in the metropolitan area.

MAP H: New Directions — 1958-1975

The latest period in the city's growth has comprised several main aspects. Peripheral expansion has continued in an arc from Howth to Killiney. Public and private housing areas have been developed separately thus lessening social contact between them. Apart from the high rise towers at Ballymun the building idiom has been largely 2 storey semi-detached or terrace housing—repetitive and unrelieved by park or greenery. The largely unchanged face of Dublin centre has suddenly been altered by the intrusion of taller buildings with a different module, using modern materials often ill at ease with older neighbouring buildings. Three new towns created to the west (Tallaght, Blanchardstown, Clondalkin) will contain most of the anticipated development over the next decade or so when the capital will contain 1 million people—nearly one quarter of the entire population of the island.

The Urban Landscape

Having looked at the city developing in history and thereby gained an appreciation of how it has been built and shaped, we can now examine it a little more closely. The city functions in many related ways — social, economic and physical — but the special theme of this chapter is the urban landscape. This consists of the design, layout, and planting of the city's buildings, districts, networks and spaces; the object is to analyse these elements in terms of what they are, how they change and the way in which they can be experienced.

Character may be in evidence in many ways — the leafiness of a city street, or the liveliness of the street traders' counters — and therefore it will be of help to consider it in a systematic way from the broad scale down to the detailed one.

The natural setting of Dublin provides it with its greatest assets. Being on the coast means ready access to the shoreline for the people, a port function to help the economy, and a seaward orientation for a large proportion of the residents. A generally flat plain has facilitated expansion in every direction and helps to focus attention on buildings rather than hills and valleys as in, say, Cork. The nearby mountains provide a visual backdrop to the southern part of the city, are a dominant element in the new south-western suburbs and provide an important recreational resource. The landscape structure helps climatically to give an open aspect and to minimize the risk of smog and persistent air pollution. For many, this aspect of Dublin as a breezy coastal city on a magnificent curved bay, is its main characteristic; the natural environment therefore is part of the Urban Landscape even though it contains it.

The major components of the city are next in scale, those areas into which the whole may be conveniently divided. When looked at in plan, it would seem that the obvious boundaries are represented by the river (cutting the city in two halves) the canals (an inner and an outer circle) or the main roads (segments radiating from the centre and the various bridges). Alternatively, an imaginary cross section through the entire urban area would show a differentiation between the taller denser built-up core and the low profile of the outer development.

These major divisions are a useful way of identifying some overall features. Your inveterate Dubliner will insist that there are decisive differences between the north side and the south side. If he hails from the south side himself, he will confess to either an ignorance of what the other side is like, or to being disoriented anywhere north of O'Connell Street. To many others, the modest span of the Liffey is not the divide, but the curving arms of the canals. Inside is the "real" Dublin — of literature, history and architecture; outside is a later addition, something not quite genuine, of nondescript character. In a motorized age, much of the city is seen when in transit, and the urban area is comprehensible solely in terms of main roads and large areas between them; only frontages are familiar — one feels that what lies behind must be more of the same!

Even the casual visitor, however, will identify much more than the foregoing. The thoughtful citizen with a more detailed knowledge of the city will have characterized it in his own mind. Like the rooms of a house, parts of the city can serve a use, have their own decor and evoke certain memories. These are the environmental areas and may be considered from the three aspects of History, Function and Identity.

1. HISTORY

Ideally, the varied history of the city should be self-explanatory from the presence of areas, however small, which typify each era in its history. But turbulent years can destroy, natural disaster can wreck, and the traces of ordinary people and their life can be easily erased. Of the city up to 1700 there is surprisingly little apart from some individual buildings. The early city has vanished, and with it part of Dublin's heritage and therefore identity. We are told the city existed even before the Vikings, but we cannot see what it was like or walk around in it. There are clues, of course, and the excavations near Christ Church have revealed Viking, Norse and medieval remains. In a sense, the roots are there, but not the stem or foliage. This evidence, below ground level and, in what is now a waste land, will soon be built upon. More than a thousand years of city form will then exist only in history books.

The Dublin of the 18th century is still readily identifiable as two complete districts: Merrion and Fitzwilliam

A.12   New buildings in mature urban landscape

A.13   Urban space severed by traffic (courtesy Bord Failte)

the spaces left are in fact private or institutional grounds rather than deliberately planned parkland.

The Outer Suburbs

Residential areas are major components of the city scene. With decentralization, lower densities and greater construction capability, the housing of the past 50 years exceeds in size the city built up to then. While there are differences in style, size and layout of these residential areas, the entire outer circle of the city presents a somewhat uniform appearance — in massing, scale and repetition. The presence of hills, mature woodland and country mansions have been obliterated or engulfed so that there are no significant landmarks, no break points, no variety except perhaps where these were impossible to absorb — Howth hill, Dun Laoghaire harbour, the Liffey valley. In terms of size and impact this is a dominant city feature now.

Port and Industry

A final major land use area is that formed by Industry and the port. In Dublin this was formerly very much restricted to the docks area, extended by railway and

squares: Mountjoy square. There are other "bits and pieces" important in themselves (like Henrietta street) or monumental buildings; but only the squares are a virtual complete untouched legacy of a size and style which is both significant and unmistakable. One can move around in them, describe their contents and see their links with previous and subsequent eras.

This period of about a century is in fact the only distinctive historical era represented in Dublin's structure. Later growth is either anonymous and hard to place, or else a small highlight in bland surroundings. While it may be resented that Dublin's glory as a city dates from a colonial period, what went before has vanished, what followed was mediocre. This is a fate shared by not a few cities the mention of whose name conjures up a strong but confined image — Leningrad; Edinburgh; Seville.

FUNCTION

Another way of looking at the city and recognising whole areas of district character is to see how it functions. As the capital city, centre of finance and commerce, a large portion of Dublin can be identified as having this use. Centralization and high land costs result in high building, repetitive units and daytime use only for these areas devoted to administration. One set of consequences is the cliff-like street walls, monotonous repetition, and a deserted air at evenings or weekends. Luckily for Dublin, this effect is somewhat dispelled by the small amount (relatively) of this development, its dispersed nature and its overlap with the 18th century districts.

Shopping for the most part is more diffused, but there are two main districts: Henry street - Talbot street and Georges street - Grafton street, in the centre city area. The keynote here is less the glass-fronted stores lining the pavements than the intensity of pedestrian traffic, its movement continuous in or out of the buildings. Interspersed are a myriad of other uses, but a few are worthy of special note, being specialist areas: riverside auction rooms; doctors "ghetto" in Fitzwilliam; cloth-trade wholesalers in south William street; booksellers near Trinity College, insurance buildings on Dame street.

Each of these areas has common characteristics, either in standard of maintenance, degree of opulence,

amount and type of associated activity: one is impressed in passing by the neatness of the consulting rooms but encouraged to pause and browse at bookseller's open racks.

Open spaces are an obvious part of the urban scene and a definite sector even though they may function in a number of ways — passive, active or decorative — or in combinations of these. Most open spaces are decorative (especially the parks) and in addition may provide for recreation. College green is an exception, being a traffic laden intersection; and yet it is also an impressive open space setting off two imposing buildings.

The squares are enclosed by buildings and many have been of psychological rather than practical use up to the present — important natural features to be viewed, but "out of bounds". Even though privately owned, their value to the public has been recognised and protected. The Phoenix park (and on a smaller scale, St. Stephen's green and Herbert park) combine all aspects. The only examples of continuous open space are the canals, the riverside and the seafront. Curiously, these three, of unequal interest (and even dereliction) along their lengths, are the subject of far-reaching proposals which could alter their character considerably or even eliminate their landscape value completely.

This scatter of varied open space is not part of a continuous system or linked to a grand design for the citizen to move through while traversing the city. It has not been matched by a similar pattern or significantly added to during the past 100 years; many of

A.15   Herbert Park—part of the Edwardian legacy

A.14   Industrial and residential areas meet

warehousing uses. It was not until comparatively recently that industry has been established westward of the city, influenced by the main transport routes (now road, not rail). The two areas are contrasting and have unexpected indirect consequences. Having a port function one block away from the city's main street is a most unusual situation which lends a great deal of interest, with the colour and movement of shipping. Even the two breakwater walls of the North and South Bull seem less an engineering necessity than an inspired shoreline walk — with an extra bonus in the creation of Dollymount strand. Much of the associated land areas are for bunkerage, with the result that heavy transporter traffic must cross the city, even through the historic district and along the open spaces. New industry is characterized by immense barnlike structures and extensive new site areas; gone is the ubiquitous smokestack, and in its place a neon-lit sign. Grimey and oppressive-looking structures have been replaced by flat grey surfaces enclosed in wire mesh fences. A new urban landscape is being created by modern industry.

IDENTITY

A third approach to viewing the city in terms of its large component parts is by identifying areas which form a single unit. One example of this idea of unity is the red brick residential streets and spaces near Dartmouth square. Although not of great historical interest or outstanding architecture, they form a consistent whole in terms of height, setback from road, maturity of vegetation, similar materials and workmanship. Other such areas are to be found around Clyde road, Elgin road, Ballsbridge, and in the vicinity of Palmerston road.

There are few similar examples on the north side but when considering the more modest proportioned houses of that and later periods many areas come to mind — the two storey red brick terrace roads off the North and South Circular roads; the split-level small-scale maze of housing near Harrington street; the cottages of the Dublin Artisans' Dwelling company in the Coombe. In many cases these were constructed by the one builder for a certain income group, a friendly society or the employees of a large industry such as Guinness or the railways.

Some of the most marked differences in urban design arise from the disparity in income. Money can buy more space, individual design, better maintenance. This is most clearly appreciated when comparing the extremes: some 100 families in Foxrock have the same space — including a golf course — as 2,000 families in Ballyfermot. In the one, tree-shaded streets, mature hedges, secluded homes forming a unique part of the city's landscape; in the other, seemingly endless streets of uniform houses, devoid of natural features.

Looked at in this way, the city is a patchwork quilt, each part with its own design: sometimes harmonizing, never dominant, but contributing to an overall effect.

Elements

The city is seldom presented in either of the foregoing ways — in its total environment or distinctive areas — but usually in terms of individual demands. This is the guidebook approach of naming or numbering a series of buildings, spaces or monuments. An obvious advantage is that by selecting the most obvious items of interest, the context too can be appreciated. But a historical note on, say, St. Stephen's church cannot explain its charm, which is partly due to its setting in a frame of 18th century houses—the contrast between the white stonework of the modelled church and the plain brick of the terraces, framing the perspective views along Merrion square and upper Mount street.

The key elements in the city do not derive solely from the obviously outstanding building or open space; they may be more subtle, like an ornate kiosk. The individual structures come most easily to mind, and their appearance is fixed in the citizen's memory: Custom House, Four Courts, Leinster House, Wellington Monument, and of course, in its time, Nelson pillar. But there are other focal points less well-known but important in their own right: the five lamps on the North Strand; the stand of trees at the top of Philipsburgh avenue or at Roebuck; the old railway viaduct over the Dodder at Milltown; Rathmines town hall; Merchants arch and the Half-penny bridge; Killiney hill and its obelisk.

Likewise with open spaces: the ones which come to mind are the great squares. In a city with a northerly clime one cannot expect the myriad and varied courtyards and terraces more suited to a sunnier or tropical

A.16 Although the township has vanished, still called Town Hall

climate. Where these spaces do occur they are, therefore, all the more surprising — the Huguenot cemetery in Merrion row as a space to be viewed, St. Patrick's park in the heart of a densely built up area; Lincoln place; the internal courtyard of Stephen Court; the sculpture garden at the Irish Life building in Mespil road; Sandymount green. Some may be private, others public but kept locked; their usefulness varies, but each is a welcome break in the building mass. One even has a continental look about it: the public convenience surrounded by trees forming a traffic island near St. Patrick's cathedral.

Certain streets have an unmistakable air about them, having a mixture of building-style and function. In the case of some — say Grafton street or Moore street — they are in no way remarkable when examined critically; but somehow they have a vitality of their own especially — or perhaps only — when in use. Harcourt terrace is one of only streets designed as an entity and even now, shorn of its trees is unique in somewhat the same way as Ely place. Griffith avenue is also in this category, being the only large scale attempt at a boulevard effect in Dublin, an example which has been repeated nowhere else. The great sweep of the bay should have afforded a great opportunity for coastal routes, but the railways got there first. The result is not flattering for the landscape of shoreline and backing hills. Most roads and streets have no particular character about them — they might be anywhere, can go unnoticed, are on the way to someplace, merely an address.

Some elements of the urban scene achieve their impact not merely by their content and style but by their relationship to each other to the street and to the viewer. Arnott street may be charming as a long terrace of one storey frontages facing each other across a narrow street lined with tiny gardens. If the street were longer like Landers road in Ballyfermot, or the houses were two storey, as in Crumlin, the effect would be completely different: monotony, oppressiveness and the exclusion of much sunlight would result. If the houses were subject to current road, pathway and setback requirements, the overall impression would be one of bleakness and isolation. Height, length and breadth are as real as concrete and trees; notice the difference

between Merrion square and Fitzwilliam square with somewhat the same ingredients. The absence of a grid-iron or chessboard pattern in Dublin means a greater variety. The curve of the Liffey both reduces its impact as a void and reveals constantly-changing patterns of riverside facades.

Natural Features

Many noteworthy elements in the city are natural features. At this scale parks, canal banks and playing fields are the main examples. They provide a contrast to the hard surfaces and geometry of buildings and roads. They recall perhaps the distant countryside or (in the downtown area) that Work is not supreme. There are the deliberate set-pieces of planting, seen at its most varied in St. Stephen's green; there are the seeming-casual but nonetheless planned efforts in places like Fairview park and Blackrock park; from unpromising situations (including reclaimed land) assets can be created. The Hill of Howth and the Phoenix park are two areas of the city where extensive and varied natural forms have been incorporated into

A.17 The largest enclosed park in the world

A.18 Sundrive—a long way from maturity

A.19 A reminder at Loughlinstown of a vanished railway

A.20 Is "concrete jungle" an unfair description?

A.21 Front gardens cannibalised by the car

the built-up areas. It is perhaps the distribution and type of natural features which favours one portion of the city or another. Sundrive park is the same size as Herbert park, yet the differences are startling — maturity, maintenance, design and equipment all favour the Ballsbridge park. Yet it serves fewer families in its immediate environs. Perhaps the fact that Dublin is at the coast, near to the mountains, with three major rivers and two broad canals, has made the need for natural features seem less urgent than in other less-well-endowed cities. But these resources could be depleted, abused or neglected without compensatory action, or their existence used as an excuse for lack of new provision.

Details
At the smallest scale of the urban scene are those details which refine what is good, humanize the mechanical and help transform the mundane. These touches are most obvious near at hand, when time is not important and the individual is most himself. For instance the choice and use of materials is most important: brick-work in large amounts can be monotonous and so it must be relieved by either ironwork (Fitzwilliam), stone facing (Merrion square) or a colour variation (Clyde road). Large surfaces need either contrasting planes (window reveals in bright plaster) or recesses.

Colour can enliven or jolt the senses: a yellow door may relieve an otherwise drab exterior but would make a whole building garish. The gasometer is acceptable in grey, and oil storage tanks look well in pastel shades — but red and white stripes on a tall chimney (supposedly necessary for aircraft safety) at once single it out for attention and over-emphasise its presence. The natural built-in colour of brick and its long usage have helped designers to handle it to good effect. Concrete, on the other hand, offers no such discipline. If used on large buildings unpainted, it may look discreet; on repetitive housing the result is deadly dull. One of the most livening features of most public housing is the individuality of the residents as displayed in their brightly painted housefronts and balconies.

2. CHANGE
One of the disturbing — or exciting — aspects of urban life is change. Dublin has evolved at a much slower

pace than many other cities. (Sao Paulo in 1900 was equal in size to Norman Dublin; it has today five times more people than the Irish capital). But a quickening tempo of new activity, replacement and alteration in familiar surroundings gives rise to concern, regret and even fear. The city we know is always changing and to a large extent is superimposed where previous man-made or natural features existed — the Coombe was once a stream bed, Donnybrook a fairgreen, St. Stephen's green a swampy wasteland, the markets area a monastery. Successive uses may appear to be for the better or for the worse: the Iveagh buildings replaced a warren of slum housing; before its banks were developed, the Dodder was a sparkling river with prime trout. Change can occur at all scales of the urban landscape. The bay and river mouth have been ordered by the sea walls and the railways.

Even more varied change would result from the present landfill proposals. A whole natural setting could be modified, this time not merely at ground level but by the creation of a new city district, a new building mass and skyline in the foreground of the bay. After a thousand years of gradual expansion to the north and south the city had suddenly expanded dramatically westwards; its previous orientation to harbour and coast will shift somewhat to the rivers and the mountains.

As new major components are added to the city, its identity will surely change — not automatically for the better. Any one of the new western suburban towns — Tallaght or Clondalkin or Blanchardstown — will have the same size and population as the whole city had by 1700. Many elements in the city have reached the limit of their useful or structural lives. Wider and faster roads are proposed where there are now streets and buildings. St. Patrick's cathedral may find itself next to a major traffic intersection roundabout. Bachelor's walk may no longer be a series of contrasting coloured facades but a dark glass and metal wall. Already there has been a noticeable change for the worse in the details and small objects which have hitherto characterised many parts of town. Door fronts and shop windows on redevelopment are often strictly private offices. Rows of gardens inside their trim railings can become the ground floor car park — concreted, stained and windy.

Lamp standards which once matched nearby railings are replaced by sleek shiny poles; textured walls and rich ornament give way to trend-seeking gimmicks. The front lawn is becoming a grass border to the enlarged driveway.

Not all change is permanent and frequently there is a cyclic effect: Mount Pleasant square was once a fashionable crescent of town houses; later the units became more valuable as bedsitters; but with new housing becoming more anonymous and more distant, that square is once again a desirable place in which to live. With a dearth of office space, once-residential streets like Wellington road are rapidly becoming a linear car park as property changes hands. Front gardens can be asphalted, railings removed and foliage cut back. These effects are more subtle than the irreversible sets of development: e.g. factories on the Dodder bank.

Very often these changes occur as the result of a not so obvious building section. The interior arrangement of rooms and ceiling heights do not fit readily into the developer's arithmetic for lettable space, and therefore demolition of whole streets becomes an economic possibility. Absentee ownership and intensive use can mean lack of maintenance, leading to lack of repair and unsound condition — sometimes in single structures, more often in whole blocks. A roadway proposal in a city plan may require land-acquisition over a period of time during which people or businesses move elsewhere, vacant structures are boarded up or demolished, and those still occupied steadily decay. Blight of this kind can be seen in Clanbrassil street and Charlemont street. The greater difficulty now met with in obtaining loans to purchase an older rather than a new house reduces the possibility of many families moving back into the older neighbourhoods. This regenerative effect is missing, and its absence together with other factors have led in Dublin, as in many cities, to an inevitable deterioration, the so called "twilight areas".

3. PERCEPTION
The point is often made that the appreciation of a good building and to a lesser extent, fine trees is purely subjective and restricted to the trained eye. It is true 13

that an architect or landscape architect can express his understanding and pleasure of these things and can let them influence his work. But the fact that many people know their environment lacks something — whether for recreation purposes or as a distinctive character — has led to unease. At times what is lacking may be precise — a children's playground — but again be no more than a vague idea of what is wrong but not what is required and to the use of emotive phrases such as "concrete jungle". This raises an important issue — the importance of the living environment. Are we affected by our surroundings? Do we respond well to pleasant greenery and badly to obsolescence?

Extravagant claims have been made both ways: that man's behaviour is determined by his environment, or that he is oblivious of it. What evidence there is suggests that the physical surroundings *by themselves* do not substantially alter behaviour: that primary needs must first be satisfied (food, shelter, security) before there is a concern for the secondary aspects (style, choice, refinement) and that there are wide variations in reaction to items like colour, proportion, texture. It seems likely, however, that a small society, observing the same norms and sharing the same traditions, has a general approach to its surroundings which is broadly similar to others of like scale.

We can examine this reaction to the urban landscape by identifying the ways in which it can be experienced, understood and used.

4. LANDSCAPE EXPERIENCE

The different senses each reveal an aspect of the city's landscape. At a first glance it would appear that sight is the only faculty used for seeing both individual buildings, groups, nearby and in vista, narrow confines and panoramas. But Dublin (at least to its detractors) is also known for its smell! The nose observes the Liffey (especially at low tide); the salt-laden air along the shoreline; the distinctive evidence of the largest brewery in the world; the more localized identities of bakery shops and the gas works. City traffic noise tends to dominante one's hearing, but there are other lesser sounds which assail the ear — church chimes, which can be distinguished from each other; the bell rung on the quays before auctions; street buskers, the cries of

newspaper boys and street traders. The tactile sense responds to cobblestones, granite and brick, iron handrails, shiny door plates.

In his book "The Image of the City", Kevin Lynch has made a systematic attempt to record the way in which people perceive their city. He found that most people identify five kinds of element:

Landmarks or focal points e.g. Ringsend chimney.
Nodes or convergence points e.g. Christchurch place.
Edges or boundary definitions e.g. the Liffey.
Barriers or obstacles/divisions e.g. the railway at Drumcondra.
Places or identifiable areas e.g. Kenilworth square.

This system certainly seems to be a valid one. It can be argued that each citizen has his own idea of the city and follows a personal set of imaginary signposts. What is important however is that the guiding elements are identifiable whether it be the "Cat and Cage" pub or the walk through Dame court. It is the lack of one or more of these sets of elements which make many new housing areas 'anonymous', 'endless', 'featureless' and so many new major buildings 'faceless'.

5. LANDSCAPE MEANING

A much more subjective and personal feeling enters in when the meaning or importance of the landscape is involved. What may be involved here is an individual's insight into what he can experience, and this is probably as variable as human nature. A sense of history could transform a person's reaction to streets and buildings: it was while strolling down Grafton street to attend his studies at Trinity College that Lord Edward Fitzgerald first saw his future wife Pamela sitting in the low window balcony which still survives; likewise with Croppies Acre, the Pidgeon House, Butterfield house — the list is endless. Booterstown avenue seems more than just a narrow winding link road when remembered as the old road from Tallaght to the sea, a cattle trail, a link between seaside villas like Frascati and the hinterland.

In a similar way, an appreciative eye can make its owner the richer by recognising good examples of craftsmanship — ironwork, moulded doorway arches,

granite curved steps, a modern bronze curtain-wall, the art of the letter painter on a fascia, carved capstones, manholes decorated with shamrocks — the accumulation of many years care, attention and mastery. The role of nature in the city can be appreciated — the way in which a profusion of planting in great variety characterizes the larger parks; the serenity of trees reflected in a canal; the softening effect of mid street planting in O'Connell street or Baggot street; the foresight which made the Phoenix park belong to the people.

These aspects and details of the city depend for their appreciation on the individual. The more alert and informed, the more sensitive to their presence. It may be unfair to compare the established features of a city with those of recently built developments; the one has been accumulated and worked on for hundreds of years, the other is an almost instant creation and inevitably lacks maturity. But something must be learned about emotional needs and responses if the newly-created environment is to be wholly satisfying to its inhabitants.

A.22 *Open space of quite inhuman scale*

A.23 *The Five Lamps*

The Physical Framework

The Coastline and the Bay
by Hugh Brady

The Liffeyside
by Reg Chandler
and Pascal Lavin

Canals and Basins
by Sean Rothery
and David Richards

The Coastline and the Bay

by Hugh Brady

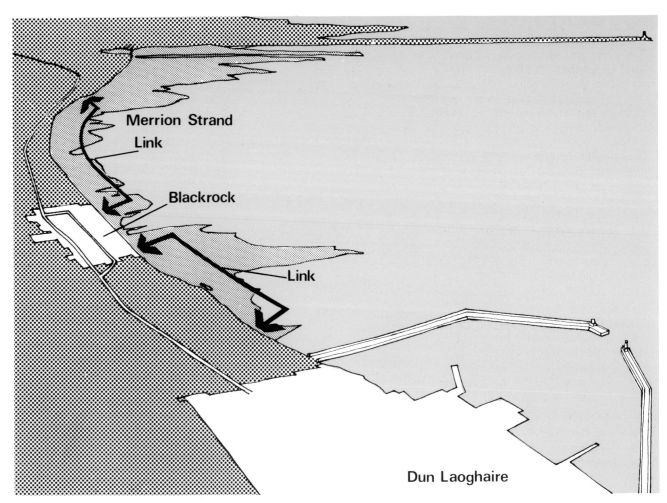

1.0   The Southside Park system

1.1   The quintessence of the Bay is its openness

The natural setting of Dublin forms the urban landscape at a city-wide scale. The shape of the bay has influenced the shape of the city itself which now extends in an uninterrupted curve from Howth to Dun Laoghaire. Landforms rising towards the extremities gives a sense of enclosure. This natural form underlines the man-made, and the mixture of landscape and architecture is an essential characteristic of Dublin. The contact between the two creates interest:

—The cliff-like prominences of tall terraces.
—The hard edges of coastal roads.
—The large tracts of wooded estates.
—The flat expanses of sand changing with the rhythmical cycle of the tides.
—The punctuation of the promontories.

This subtle blend of both the natural and built environments can be appreciated in the pattern of lights at night which continue to express the form and scale of the Bay even when the natural features are no longer visible.

Citizens think of the Bay as an entity, a singular possession like, say, the Phoenix Park. But their bay is perceived in this way only when seen from the mountains, at Dalkey or Howth. From a lower viewpoint or from within the built-up area the whole bay cannot be seen or at least grasped.

The quintessence of the bay is its openness.

It may be that because land uses are approximately symmetrical around the Bay that the citizens of one side can see the problems of their counterpart visited upon them. For example residents of Clontarf are not only concerned about port reclamation close to the Fairview shore but also fear what may happen if the port activities are consolidated all the way to Sandymount strand—a proposal viewed with equal mistrust by south side bay residents. Both communities may well equate the presence of amenity with the absence of buildings—the prospect is pleasing.

Change in the city itself may have virtually no impact on the bayside dweller: the city proper is always on the edge of vision, the docks merge into the city. So it is only what happens in the bay or along its edge that seems to matter.

Tower blocks in Sutton (or at Merrion) would have to be quite tall in order to register. Such a suggested radical change tends to provoke bay-wide objection: but just as the natural forms dominate at Howth and Killiney, there is a strong case that man-made forms should provide landmarks or focal points of interest where the landscape is flat, featureless and unrelieved.

The city and the bay are related as to function: one influencing the other.

The inner part of the bay—the Port Area—poised, awaiting the outcome of the debate on its future; but the process of change continues, hastened by the effects of neglect and uncertainty. Maintenance is discontinued, older buildings decay; dereliction spreads; in the face of deteriorating environment people move out; houses are provided elsewhere and job patterns alter due to a shift in industrial location. As a consequence, parish units become islands separated by empty areas of yards and warehousing or divided by traffic routes.

1.2   The whole bay can only be seen from the hills

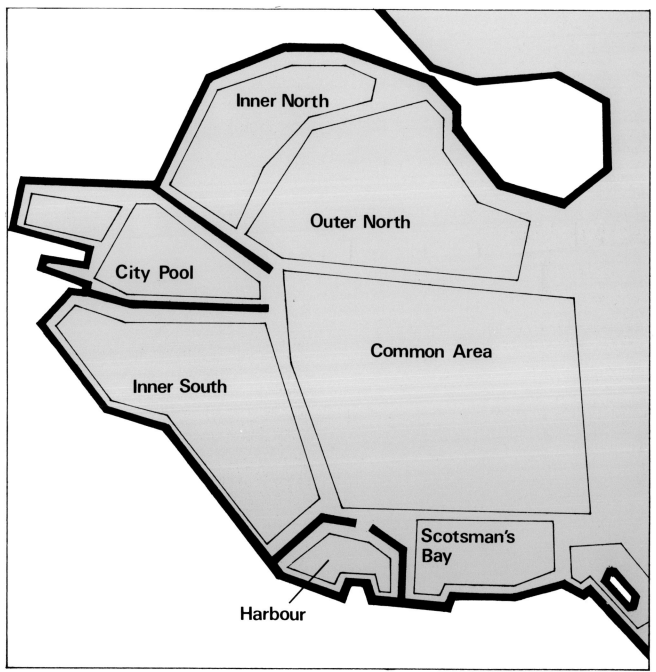

1.3   The separate "bays" the citizens know

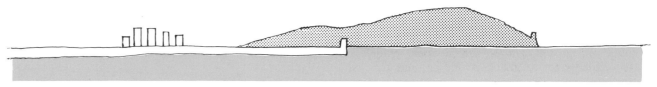

1.7   *The effect of very high towers at Sutton would be slight in comparison*

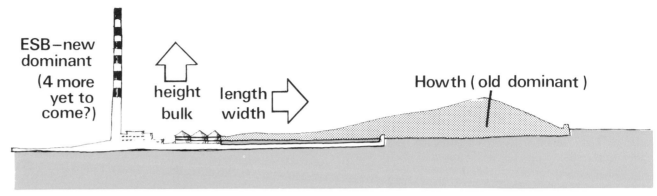

ESB–new dominant (4 more yet to come?)

height bulk ⬆

length width ➡

Howth (old dominant)

1.5   *Industry becoming progressively intrusive*

1.4   *The air-traveller's view*

The other parts of the bay are the recipients of recent change, as the growth of car ownership stretches the convenient or practical distance between home and work. In the intervening areas, the more settled suburbs of yesteryear, the natural landscape is subdued but not dominated by the man-made. These suburbs are no longer considered as 'desirable': deterioration spreads from the centre, housing stock grows old, the skyline is encroached upon by industry. Through traffic, en route from extremities to centre, makes increasing demands on residential streets, creating conflicts in which the residents are the main if not the only sufferer.

Change must be dealt with—the bay area is lived in and not merely looked at; but what seems to be merely a local change may have wide repercussions elsewhere.

The geometry of the bay is such that some parts of it are constantly in view. But the scale is such that only major features stand out, and the port is the only intrusion on all views across this focal point.

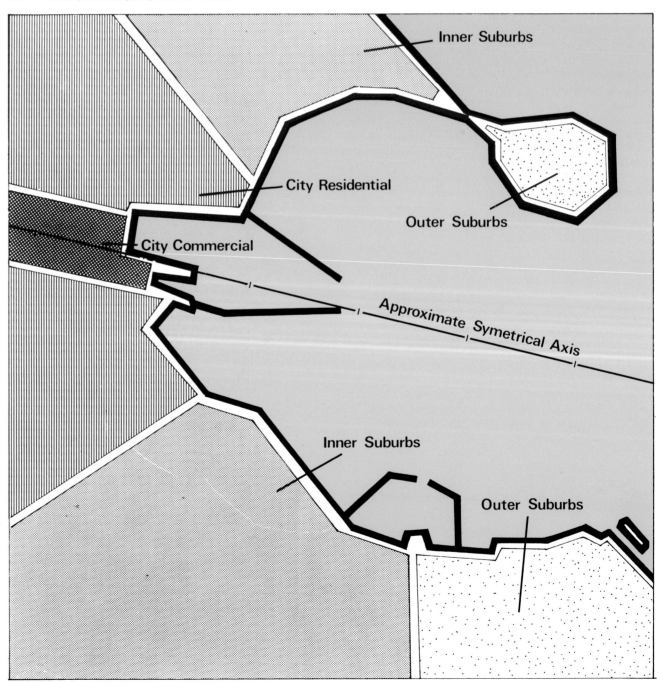

Inner Suburbs

City Residential

Outer Suburbs

City Commercial

Approximate Symetrical Axis

Inner Suburbs

Outer Suburbs

     1.6   *Symmetrical land uses around the Bay*

Port development. The larger it grows the more it obscures the background: the farther out it expands, the more it dominates the focal point in the bay. Even if policies of growth can be agreed upon, guidelines will be required for height, bulk, colour, and the rest.

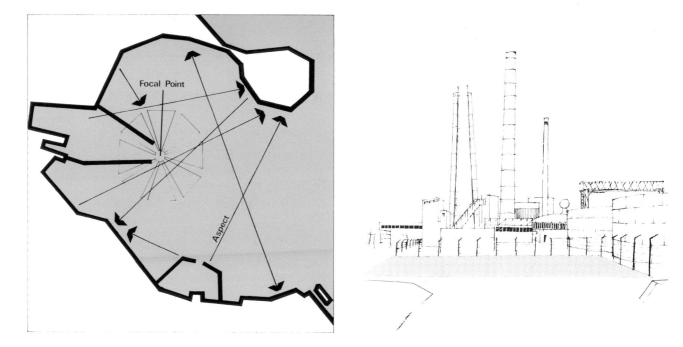

The Bay — Opportunities

A unique characteristic of Dublin Bay must be the ability to travel right around the city without losing sight of the water. This asset—seen at its most dramatic in a city like Rio De Janeiro—can be realized to the full, to everybody's benefit.

Some of the elements are already there and, given imaginative treatment, could be transformed. A few of these can be presented.

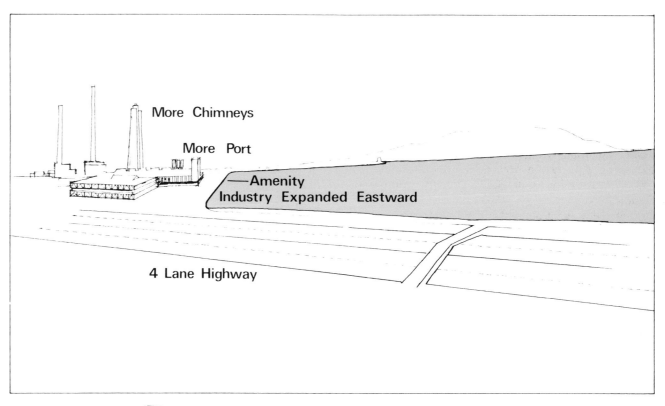

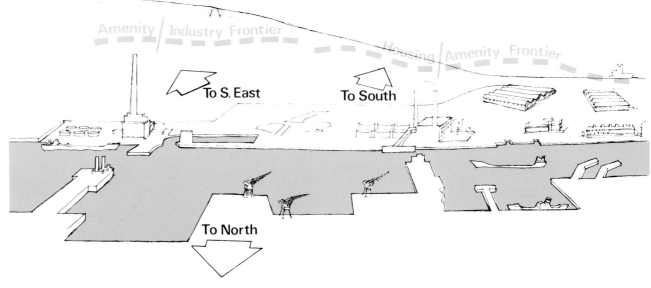

1.8.   *Further port expansion is planned*

Northside Shoreline. The northside park system is essentially a flat strip of land. Its long linear shape has little variety in visual experience and recreational use.

To improve this situation, certain areas could be developed as nodes providing such facilities as windbreaks, access structures to the bay, small court games, and sheltered seating.

In the area adjacent to the North Bull bird sanctuary, a visual and physical separation should be developed with the intention of enhancing the bird sanctuary, which needs protection from intrusion, and yet creating enough openness for bird observation. The park abutting the Clontarf and James Larkin road should have a continuous park development so that it would link Fairview park with St. Anne's park.

1.9   North shore—suggested landscaping

1.10   Coastline north

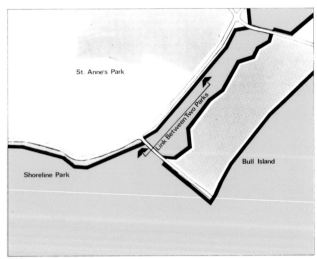

1.11   The Northside park system

South Side. The Southside park system is basically well developed, but there are tremendous pressures from intensive use by the public and from surrounding development. To relieve some of this public pressure, certain areas within each park could be strengthened by better circulation control and more use of well-detailed hard surfaces in each activity area.

Footpaths as illustrated would link the separate park areas and would help to dissipate the crowded conditions. These footpaths would be similar to the existing ones in that they could be located either inside or outside the sea defence wall.

There are proposals for a new motorway which will cater for major traffic flows along the seafront at Sandymount-Merrion. The intention is to lower the carriageway below ground level on a line parallel to the present Strand road. A strip of park would then be contained between the existing and and the proposed road.

The scale of the new motorway would dominate the existing buildings and in effect move the residents inland. The road user would have no view of the bay as it would be above eye level—except from the top of a bus. The park would become an isolated strip between roadways, requiring protective barriers to the motorway and thus prevent easy access to the strand. The possibilities of success in handling such major elements for the benefit alike of resident and passer-by are very limited. A deeper cutting for the new roadway would lessen noise, facilitate more direct pedestrian access, minimize the intrusion of tall lighting fixtures. Landscaping the road corridor itself would compensate for the loss of seaward views and enliven the journey. Creating activity nodes at certain points in park together with land shaping and planting would increase the capacity for recreation, provide wind breaks and introduce a new note of vitality.

Responding to new proposals for roadways begs the question: are they needed, must they be here, who benefits, what are the costs, have alternatives been considered, who decides? Action should depend on the nature of the answers—the case for a coast motorway has not yet been made; its potential impact has serious consequences; there are inland options for a route: there is only one coastline.

Approaches to the Bay

The city during most of its history developed on the river banks and only in later times has it reached out to the shoreline. There has been no conscious architectural style along the seafront—with the notable exception of the terraces from Seapoint to Dun Laoghaire—and no deliberate attempt made as yet to create a distinctive bayside environment. These opportunities will provide a challenge to future designers, particularly if there is choice as to density, massing and civic spaces.

In evolving a 'personality' for development along the bay the junction between city and bay is important. On the northside, the transition is marked by the railway line; the bridge forms a gateway. Just as in a doorway, one is conscious of a definite change from the inside (city) to the outside (bay). Such experiences help to define the major elements in the city and relieve monotony. The impact has been lessened by the advancing land-fill which has reduced the open aspect when viewed from the west and by the diminishing width of water which results in a greater sense of closure as one travels from east to west.

It is essential therefore to retain the water barrier between industry and residence. The separation—at the narrowest stretch between the two—can be reinforced by screen planting in what is the most sheltered part of the Clontarf waterfront.

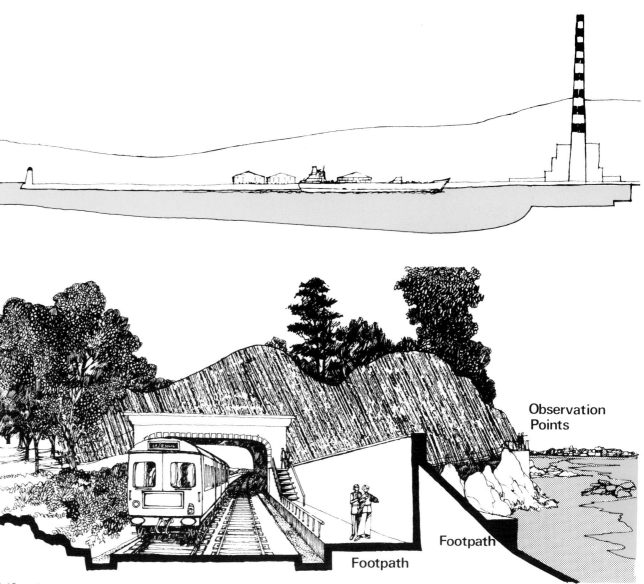

1.13 Coastline south and motorway proposals

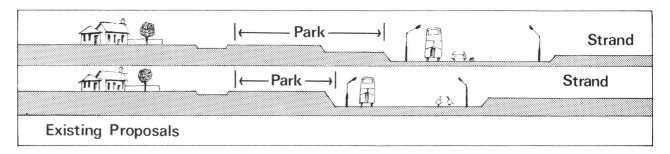

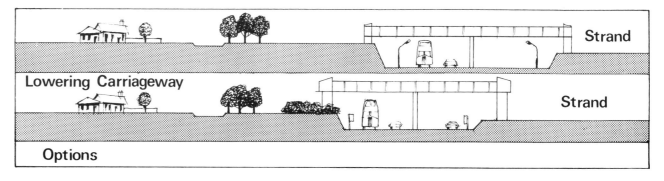

On the south side the transition between the closed city and the open bay is not as distinct. There is the same feeling of exhilaration as the sweep of the bay is revealed travelling southwards and the sense of gradual closure when going in the opposite direction.

Again it is vital that the water barrier remain. The transitional area—between Ringsend and Beach road —now rather featureless and derelict—needs more identity. This could be provided by some landmark or landscape dominant which would emphasise its 'gateway' role.

The other important junction between city and bay occurs in the port area both north and south of the Liffey. East Wall and Ringsend are housing areas which adjoin industry and warehousing. There are no simple boundary lines between them: a church adjoins the canal basin, coal-yards abut terrace houses, sail boats are moored beside derelict sites. Despite the seeming lack of order, there are many obvious advantages in people being near to work and close to the city and part of a small community. But there is also the pollution, constant heavy traffic and obsolete buildings to contend with. If people are to remain, there should be no lessening of standards compared to other parts of the city. In practice, this might only come about creating districts which are large enough to withstand encroachment, with a range of facilities to be self sufficient and an environment which will satisfy its community. A growth-centre approach could be adopted—for instance offices and services could be deliberately encouraged to locate there, and the process of revitalization would soon make its impact in visual terms too.

Shaping the Bay

The shallow nature of the bay has posed a problem— how to provide satisfactory water depths for shipping —and solved another—how to create significant areas of flat land. The construction of the walls of the North and South Bulls enabled boats to use a deepened river channel, while landfill proceeded apace utilizing the city's waste.

As the pace of change quickens, increased demands arise: deeper berthage, more wharfage, extensive land. Links are established between certain industries and port activities—and more are sought. The city is faced with the prospect of an oil refinery: Is this the logical conclusion of a process already under way, or the unacceptable face of industrialization?

The issues here involve national and regional policy as do many factors in the proposed expansion of the port. The Dublin Bay Amenity Study* assessed the land needs for port-related activities, and concluded that consolidation of the present landfill and better use of derelict areas would be adequate. This could be done without affecting the level of amenity in the bay. Even without major land expansion, the present 'uneasy' relationship between industry and housing or port activities and recreation must be resolved. The creation of Dollymount Strand after the North Bull had been built is a fortuitous but happy example of utility and amenity in harmony. It should be possible to provide similar seaside leisure opportunities adjacent to the South Bull.

*Dublin Bay Amenity Study for Dublin Corporation and Dun Laoghaire Corporation, Brady, Shipman, Martin, 1974.

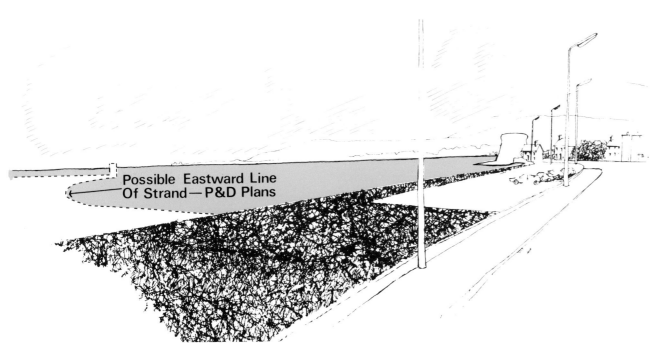

Possible Eastward Line Of Strand—P&D Plans

1.14   Approach to bay going south

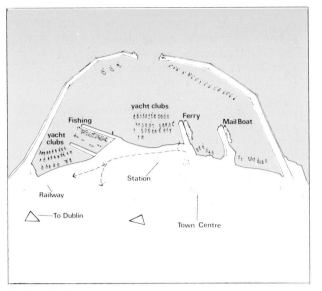

1.15   Dun Laoghaire

The Bay is a prime outlet for outdoor recreation, both informal and organized, for the population of the whole metropolitan area. An estimate in the Amenity Study suggests that 150,000 people are recreating in the bay area on a typical Sunday afternoon in summer. The situation is not static: pressure for use is shifting from the inner to the outer bay areas; organized activities such as boating are rapidly increasing in popularity; competition is growing for on-shore and off-shore space and utilities; the quality and quantity of facilities is not keeping pace with demand and interest.

Many of these factors are illustrated by the situation in Dun Laoghaire, where the original public works programme now encompasses an enormous variety of activities. The foresight, engineering skills and stone-masons' craft which fashioned the harbour more than a hundred years ago provided well for the needs of its day and created a superb setting. A point is now being reached where it can no longer provide adequately for the number, scale and nature of the demands being placed on it. Port functions now subordinate to residential dormitory suburb and sporting uses, proposed increase in port activity and associated industry. In particular, an increase in commercial ferry traffic could seriously upset balance between industrial amenity and residential uses that exists at present.

Once again the conclusion is clear: neither the bay in its man-made or natural features nor the pressures for use are static. The essential characteristics of the bay must be identified and retained; the requirements of the demand should be met as far as these capabilities allow.

Jurisdiction
One of the complications with regard to planning for the bay is the complex boundaries of ownership and of jurisdiction.

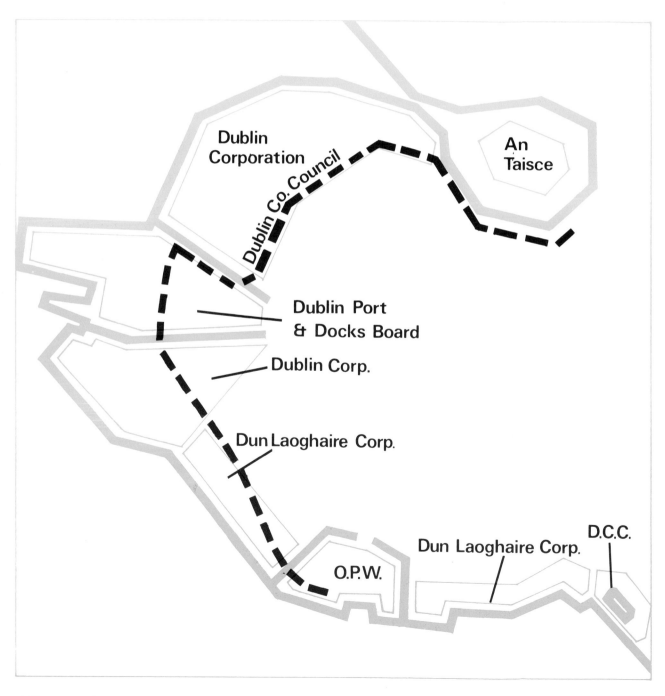

1.16   Areas of jurisidction are fragmented

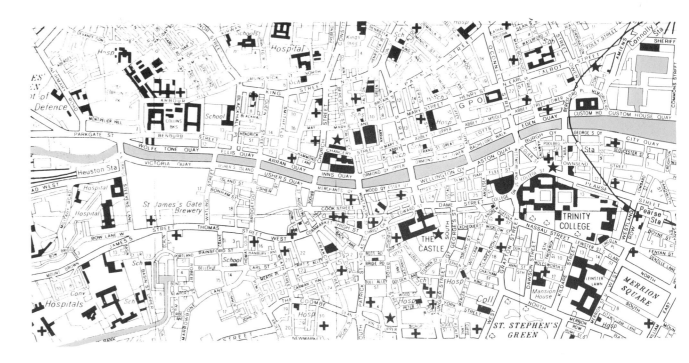

The Liffeyside

by Reg Chandler and Pascal Lavin

Historical Background

The quays, as we know them, are apparently the remains of what was created in the middle to the late 18th century. Before this, the quays consisted of timber structured wharfs built out over an ill-defined Liffey. A Malton print published in 1751 shows a river wall, with buildings more reminiscent of small buildings in Amsterdam than typical Dublin. These do not seem to have survived at all and may indicate the influence of Flemish workmen in Dublin at the time. Certainly, in the early part of the 18th century, the river was being used for docking and berthing up as far as Wood quay, although pressure was even then evident for this traffic to be moved eastward.

During the 17th century, the old walled city of Dublin had commenced to develop and extend in three directions: north along Capel street, east along both sides of the river and south-east towards St. Stephen's green. The initial development derived from private enterprise and speculation, guided here and there by vice-regal limits and municipal enactments. The

2.1 *The great seam of the city*

2.3   *When the pedestrian still was king*

demands of a growing economy and increasing trade and commerce prompted expansion.

Apart from some wharves and warehouses, the general character of the expansion was upper-class residential. A vice-regal limit of particular significance for the future development of the Liffey quays was the case where the Duke of Ormond persuaded the developer of the Essex bridge (formerly Grattan bridge) and associated warehouses and residential buildings on the north bank of the river to interpose a stone quay between the river and the new buildings, as the proposed plans showed the rears of the buildings facing the river.

By the end of the 18th century, the city had assumed its modern shape, with quays and circular roads. The city corporation leases in, for example, Aston quay (mid 18th century) obliged the lessee to leave a quay 40′ wide and to build houses in a regular and uniform manner at least three storeys high, besides cellars, the first or shop storey to be nine feet high, the second or middle storey to be ten feet high and the third to be eight feet high. This brief specification, apart from emphasising the importance of the first floor, set the pattern for the regularity of the skyline along the quays.

The Present
The list of occupiers on the quays does not show freehold ownerships; further research would be necessary on this. Dublin corporation owns a great deal of the property, but other head interests are difficult to disentangle.

Many of the buildings on both sides of the river are not fully occupied and often only contain ground floor use. This is not only true of the quays but of a large amount of the city north of the Liffey as a whole.

Visual Quality
The river represents a great seam joining the north and south sides of the city along opposite quays. This impression is visually reinforced by the proximity of the opposite sides of the river and the frequency of bridges. But from the photographs it will be seen that considerable decay exists. The Georgian quality of the South quay is almost totally gone, and in fact

2.2   *Transport problems on a different scale to now*

| Existing shops with storage & offices over | New residential over shops, small offices, restaurants, etc | Existing offices | New club | Existing offices | New residential over artists' & craftsmen showrooms & studios |

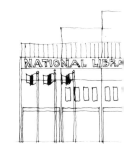

ORMOND QUAY LOWER—NORTH SIDE

2.4   *The Liffey is a unique asset, the spinal cord of Dublin*

the resultant visual environment is far from attractive. Even the visual quality of section of the North quays are unpleasant and can be much improved upon. It is proper to say that most people when talking of the quays have in mind a picture of the North quays — primarily Bachelors' Walk and the Ormond quays — bathed in sunshine (the South quays get little or no sun). This reinforces the point made by Brian Hogan in his paper on Tall Buildings, which also stresses the importance of orientation from the point of view of visual design, especially when the buildings in question are tall or otherwise prominent in location.

Planning Policy

The Liffeyside, in common with the rest of the inner city, is in a crisis situation at present. There has been a radical drop in population in the area. Industry is moving out and excessive commercial and roadway development is causing social and physical disruption. This is resulting in a city desert after working hours, with few thriving central communities remaining.

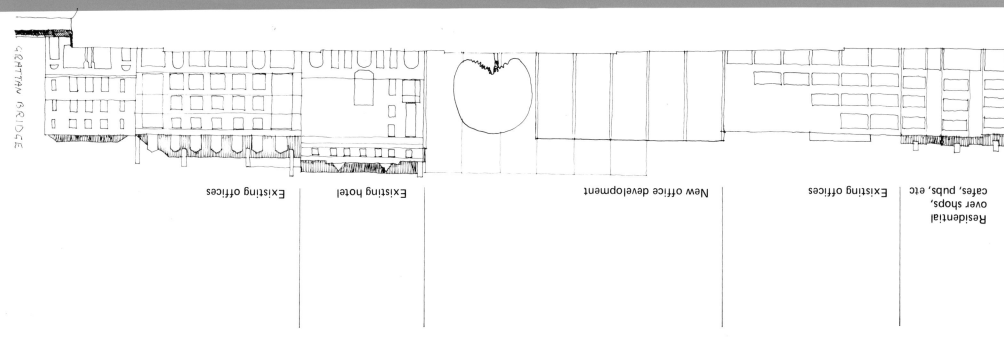

| Residential over shops, cafes, pubs, etc | Existing offices | New office development | Existing hotel | Existing offices |

Proposed site for new civic building | Shops, auctioneers' showrooms with storage etc overhead

THE 'HALFPENNY' BRIDGE

PEDESTRIAN & SEATING AREA

The development proposals which follow attempt to combine capital city establishments with the needs of ordinary people, employment possibilities and decent housing. These policies should be applied to the whole inner city as well as the Liffey quays.

Instead of the single-use zoning in the present development plan, the quays should be developed so as to provide the greatest possible variety or mix of activities with the emphasis on residential accommodation. Thus a *living area* could be created, an area remaining alive after normal working hours, composed of the activities of the local residents and the variety of recreational, entertainment and cultural activities available.

An interesting example for future development already exists in the case of Crampton quay, which, although visually insignificant, is nevertheless a lively pocket of residential accommodation, arranged round an open courtyard (Crampton court) over ground floor shops which face onto the quay. This example should be repeated along both sides of the river. The size of

2.5   *Once threatened, temporarily reprieved, must be preserved*

WELLINGTON QUAY—SOUTH SIDE

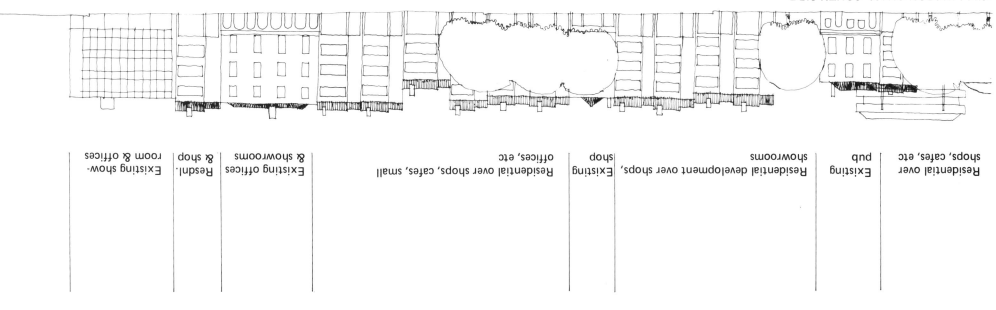

Residential over shops, cafes, etc	Existing pub	Residential development over shops, showrooms	Existing shop	Residential over shops, cafes, small offices, etc	Existing offices & showrooms	Resdnl. & shop	Existing showroom & offices

Residential over shops, auctioneers showrooms, restaurant, small offices, etc

Night club	Residential over artists/craftsmen showrooms & studios

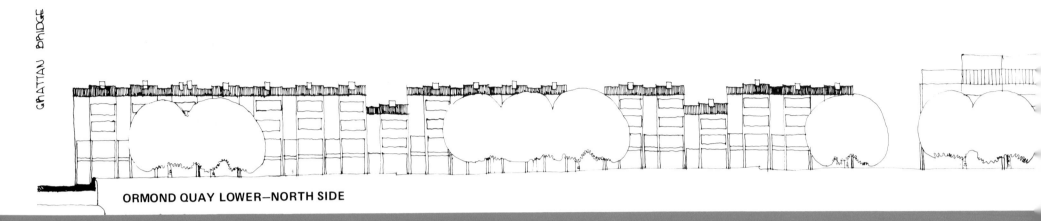

GRATTAN BRIDGE

ORMOND QUAY LOWER—NORTH SIDE

the development should be kept small in scale and restricted in height so that major civic buildings dominate.

At street level there should be a proliferation of small shops, showrooms, a few pubs, and the like. Restaurants and night clubs should also be encouraged to open up along the quays. The vast tourist potential of the area should be fully exploited. Above ground level there should be at least three floors of accommodation, comprising either residential or small offices for solicitors and similar professions.

A pilot scheme of studio workshops to accommodate artists and craftsmen with residential accommodation overhead should be undertaken on a modest scale. This would, if successful, boost the tourist potential of the area and should merit Bord Failte grants in the form of subsidised rents.

The problems of heavy traffic conflicts with the pleasures of walking along the quays. A transportation policy for the whole city, involving some form of restrictions along the quays, is required to deal with this issue. In the meantime, a programme of tree planting, particularly along the North quays, should be implemented.

An allied problem in relation to walking along the quays, is the Liffey smell which will have to be eliminated, and in this context, it is claimed that the current Dublin Drainage Scheme will eliminate the major pollution problem in the river by re-directing the Camac river through the drainage system. This will probably go some way towards alleviating the bad smell; but the only satisfactory long-term solution is the ultimate construction of a barrage with permanent ponding of the central city reaches of the river.

Finally, a riverside walkway along the north quays is proposed with steps down from path level at frequent intervals. This walkway could be enjoyed independently of street traffic; it would also have the effect of narrowing the river, thereby increasing the water flow. The increased volume of water flowing in the river combined with the results of the Dublin Drainage Scheme hopefully might eliminate the Liffey smell for good.

> *" To Dublin town I went one day*
> *and crossed the river Liffey,*
> *And by the odour of that same*
> *I knew it in a jiffy."*

(Edwardian music-hall song. Things have not changed in threequarters of a century.)

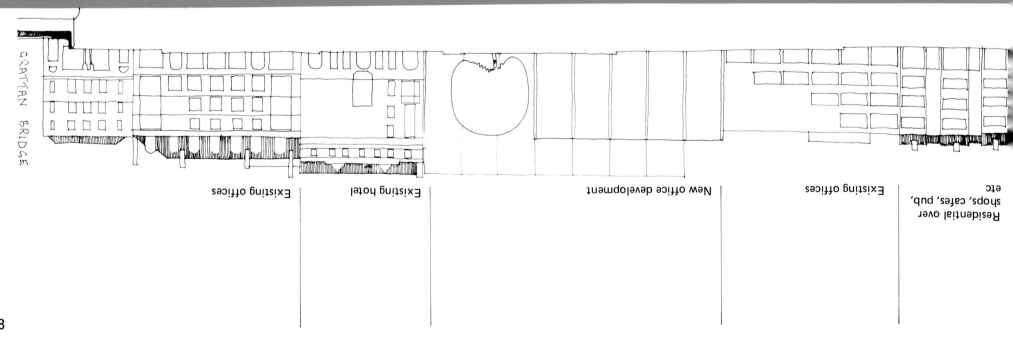

GRATTAN BRIDGE

Residential over shops, cafes, pub, etc | Existing offices | New office development | Existing hotel | Existing offices

Proposed site for new civic building | Proposed site for new civic buildings (arts centre, concert hall)

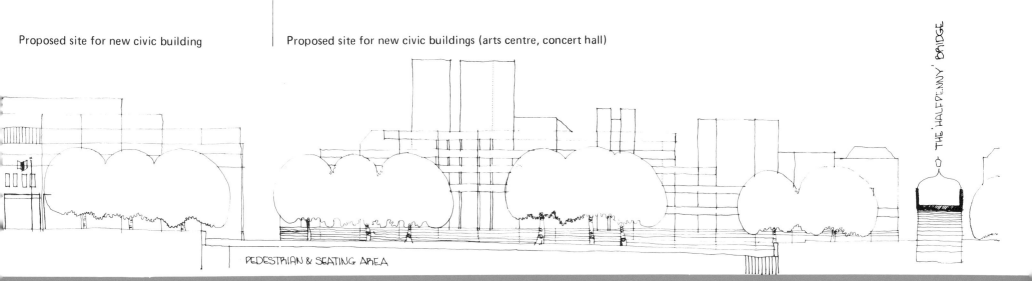

PEDESTRIAN & SEATING AREA

THE HALFPENNY BRIDGE

2.6   *Re-development is half-hearted and intermittent*

Summary and Conclusions

The study has been confined to the quays between O'Connell bridge and Father Mathew bridge.

The river presents one of the widest and most important vistas in the city.

The scale and texture of the buildings containing these vistas should be maintained.

Larger buildings, of civic or physical importance, either with or without open spaces, should be allowed to punctuate the general small scale of development in selected locations.

The amenity potential of the area should be enhanced by cleaning up the river, controlling its level and providing a new riverside walkway below the present pavement line.

The present user mix should be maintained and, preferably, extended. There should specifically be a policy decision to include housing development or re-development along both north and south quays.

WELLINGTON QUAY—SOUTH SIDE

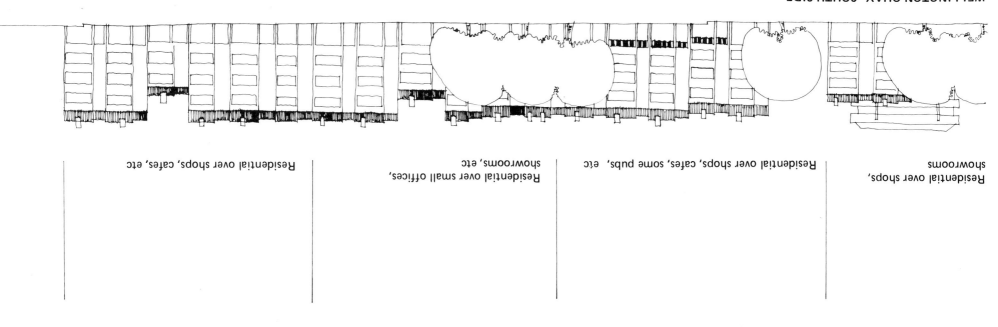

Residential over shops, cafes, etc | Residential over small offices, showrooms, etc | Residential over shops, cafes, some pubs, etc | Residential over shops, showrooms

Canals and Basins

by Sean Rothery
and
David Richards

The Royal and Grand canals, enclosing the inner city, form very dominant elements in the Dublin urban landscape. The city has long expanded far beyond the limits of the canals and since the canals themselves are now under threat from transportation planning, it is imperative to evaluate their present role and potential contribution to the townscape of Dublin.

Present Status and Uses: Grand Canal

The Grand canal now appears to have a more secure future, since the main drainage scheme is contained in a deep tunnel beside the channel and the waterway itself is not immediately threatened with abandonment. The canal is already used on occasions as a waterway by recreational craft, even within the city limits, and it is sensible to assume that with the steady growth of the inland waterway industry that this use will increase in the future. The Grand canal dock is seldom used by shipping, although still open; but the entrance locks are in poor condition. From Mount Street bridge to Portobello bridge, the canal is an important amenity and contributes in a major way to the character of the south city. There are now a number of prestige office developments along the canal-side, and the trend is obviously towards renewal and improvement, the attraction of the waterway being the main motivating factor. Further stretches of the canal towards Inchicore have been improved and cleaned and some developments, industrial and commercial, are properly related to the waterway. The spur of the Grand canal to James' harbour, which was the original start of the canal, is abandoned and very badly polluted, neglected and threatened with closure. From Inchicore to Clondalkin the canal is attracting attention from local residents, who recognise the recreational potential of the waterway. The landscape here is industrial, unplanned and largely a wasteland. Beyond Clondalkin the canal enters the country, is more frequently used by pleasure craft and is an extraordinarily beautiful waterway with occasional small gems of architecture and craftsmanship along the way — villages, stone bridges, lock-keepers' cottages, lock details and kerbing. All these areas are linked by at least one walkable towpath and footpath

GRAND CANAL 1

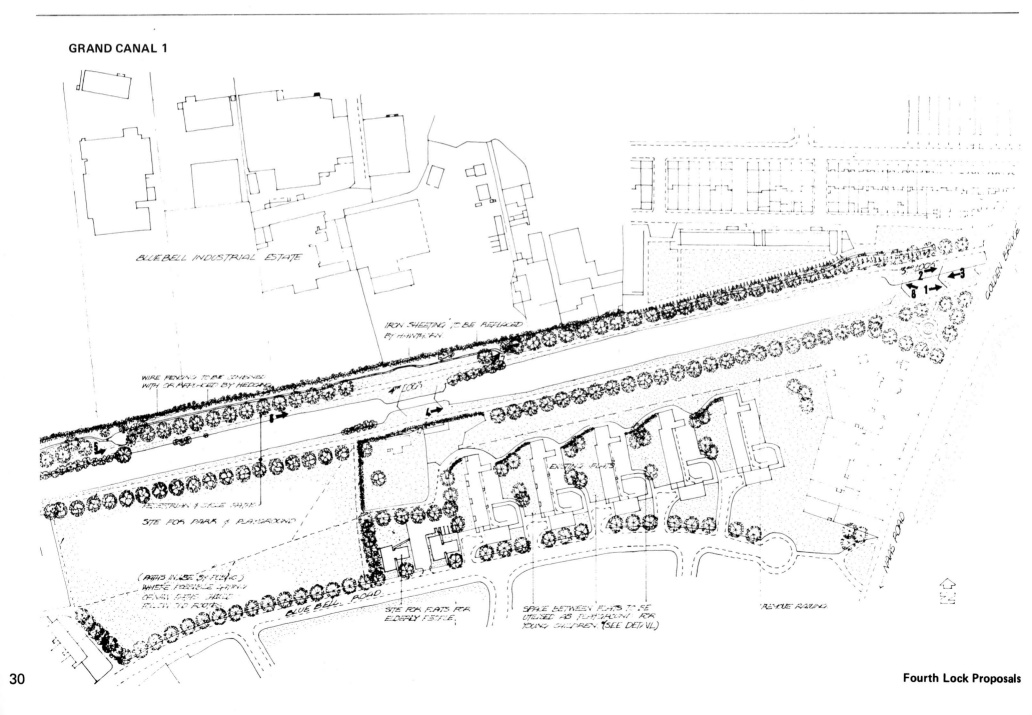

Fourth Lock Proposals

3.1 *The Grand Canal—a unique and precious linear park*

from the entrance to the Grand canal on the lower Liffey.

The Royal Canal

The Royal canal had, within a few years of its opening, strong competition from the railway which runs alongside it for most of its length. It never prospered as a commercial waterway and fell into disuse, since pleasure boating did not follow on after the commercial use ended, as happened with the Grand canal. Within the city limits, the waterway is neglected and polluted in many places, with lock gates broken and unserviceable. However, local residents' associations are becoming interested in the recreational potential, and clean-up campaigns and restoration proposals are under way. In the outer suburbs, such as Blanchardstown and Clonsilla, major clean-up programmes of the canal and clearing of towpaths are in progress, and C.I.E. is restoring locks and filling the channels. Urban renewal or office developments have not followed the line of the Royal canal as has happened with the Grand.

TREES TO PROVIDE SCREENING FROM FACTORIES - CHESTNUT. E.M. BEECH. OAK SYCAMORE.

SILVER BIRCH 'WEEPERS'

CORRUGATED IRON FENCING VERY SHABBY - TO BE REPLACED BY HEDGES & SHRUBS TO ENCOURAGE NATURE. MIXTURES OF HAWTHORN. HOLLY. WHITEBEAM & ELDER TO BE USED.

5. MILL RACE.

8. 3RD LOCK PROPOSALS

Proposals: Grand Canal

The main proposals which will affect the Grand canal are associated with the large-scale transportation plans for Dublin. The largest of these is the proposal for a multiple intersection over the dock at Ringsend. This could completely change the character of the townscape here, and unless the supports for an elevated roadway were carefully sited the waterway's use could be diminished or even blocked. Other proposals appear to envisage wide motor roads on either side of the canal for some stretches in the city. This would be disastrous for the area between Mount Street bridge and Leeson street, as the townscape here is almost perfect, with water and trees in complete harmony with the terraces and newer office buildings related to the canal.

Proposals: Royal Canal

The Royal canal motorway plan appears to accept that the Royal canal within the city limits will be closed and filled in for a large roadway which will connect with the south city motorway proposals by a new bridge across the Liffey. As with the Grand canal sewer, this proposal must be re-appraised urgently, before commitment to this route for the northern motorway becomes irrevocable.

Potential: Grand Canal

Urban renewal within the inner city has been accepted as not only desirable but essential to preserve old-established city communities and revitalize the city. The Grand canal dock offers large-scale potential for a massive redevelopment using the waterway pool as a focus. The dock itself could become a marina, and a land use study could show possibilities for large-scale housing and mixed development all around.

The present trend for new developments along the canal will undoubtedly continue; but new developments should recognise the waterway as a strong element, and each development should relate architecturally to the canal. Portobello harbour, which was filled in as a car park in recent years, offers a chance for a smaller-scale but potentially important contribution to an improved townscape for this part of the

3.2   The magic of trees and water

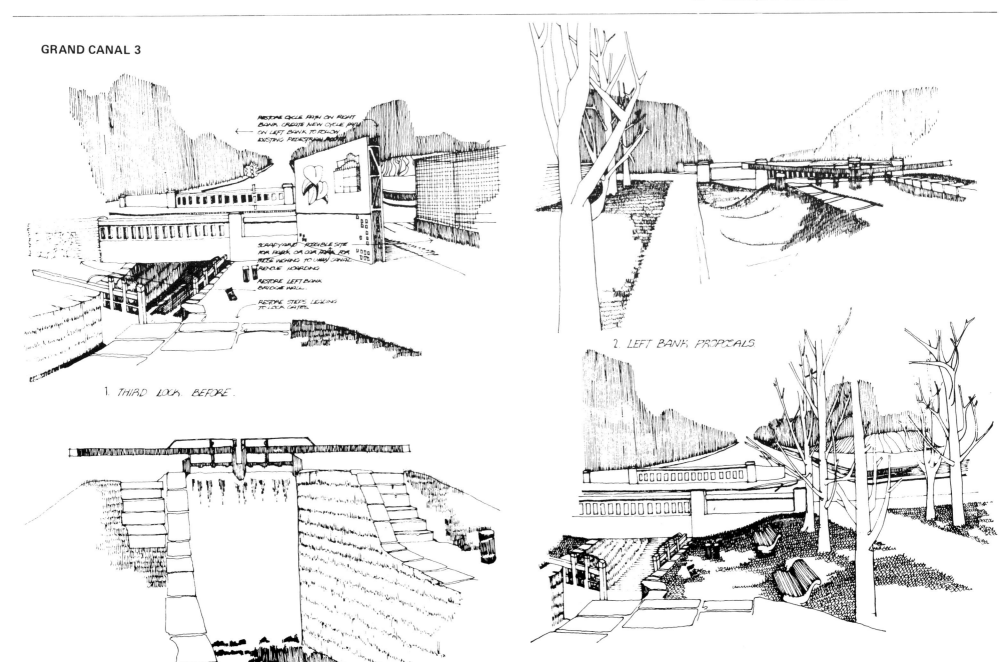

GRAND CANAL 3

1. THIRD LOCK. BEFORE.

2. LEFT BANK PROPOSALS.

3. THIRD LOCK RESTORED

1. RIGHT BANK PROPOSALS.

Third Lock Proposals

city. The old hotel has been successfully restored, and a chance exists to re-open the harbour and develop around the old area of the harbour, with the water as a major element.

James' Harbour

This stretch of the canal has been abandoned as a waterway; but rather than have the channel filled in and planted over, it would be more valuable to consider making the waterway clean and safe. This can be done by reducing the depth overall and filling the edges to an even angle with stones and gravel. The harbour could be restored and redevelopment could be carried out here, related to the water. The waterway itself and the harbour have potential for small-scale recreational boating, with footbridges connecting the two banks.

Potential: The Royal Canal

The Grand canal is universally recognised as a major environmental feature of the south city: the Royal canal, which is an equally important element, can become an axis of urban renewal on the north side.

3.3   The Royal Canal, more neglected, has perhaps even more potential

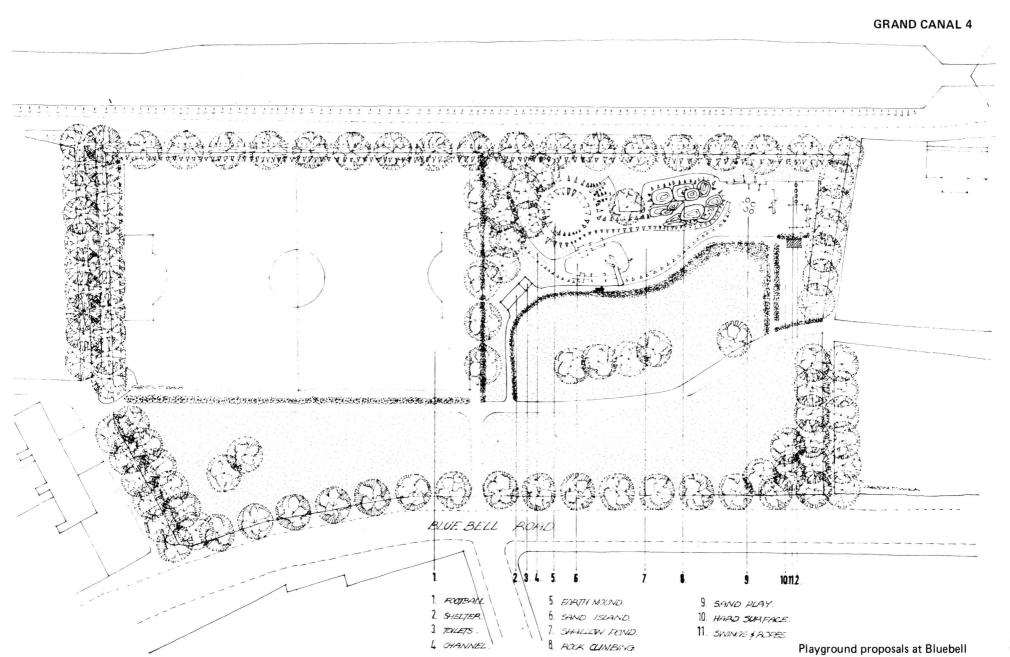

BLUE BELL ROAD

1. FOOTBALL
2. SHELTER
3. TOILETS
4. CHANNEL
5. EARTH MOUND
6. SAND ISLAND
7. SHALLOW POND
8. ROCK CLIMBING
9. SAND PLAY
10. HARD SURFACE
11. SWINGS & ROPES

Playground proposals at Bluebell

The fact that a "line of opportunity" exists for a roadway development must not be allowed to preclude a detailed study of the potential of the waterway for this renewal, apart from its obvious potential as a linear park which contributes valuable open space to large areas of nearby housing. The extra space resulting from the presence of the railway alongside the city stretch of the canal, and the availability of many potential re-development sites along the waterways, offer the possibility of an imaginative plan which would preserve the waterway and the towpaths, and provide new landscaped spaces relating to housing and commercial development. The rail service could be expanded so as to reduce the commercial traffic in the area and an improved road (less elaborate than the proposed motorway) could be designed in conjunction with the linear development plans. The Spencer dock area offers wide possibilities for housing renewal, with landscaped spaces related to the waterway. As well as improving the local environment this would also be in sympathy with the need to preserve the existing communities.

3.4   The charm of buildings and water

Conservation and Preservation

There are many arguments for and against systems of grading buildings. The simplest system would appear to be the most effective. The policy would be best based on a distinction between "preservation" and "conservation" and on a wish to encourage urban renewal rather than inhibit it. "Preservation" means the retention of a structure in its existing state or restoration to its former state and appropriate use.

Along the canals, only the churches and possibly Portobello House would come into this category along with a few significant terraces of houses which give distinctive character. "Conservation" accepts degrees of change, provided this is sympathetic to existing character and retains good design standards. Many areas along the canal can be recommended for conservation as they have a strong and distinctive character and an architectural quality. This quality is good rather than masterly; its merit lies less in the architecture than in overall unity and in a pleasant quality of scale and urbanity.

GRAND CANAL 5

New planting

Percy Place, on the Grand canal, although of no great architectural merit, has exceptional unity of composition and distinction in scale and texture, and merits particularly careful treatment. Part preservation where this is essential, careful conservation of the remainder, would seem to be the solution.

Warrington Place and **Herbert Place,** which form a portal to and define the edge of the space of Mount street crescent and frame the view of St. Stephen's church from Huband bridge, are particularly important to preserve, being an essential part of a significant view. Other important terraces on the Grand canal are those of Wilton place and Mespil road, forming an appropriate foil and contrast to adjoining modern office blocks.

Ontario Terrace, near Portobello bridge, set back behind a noble screen of trees and complete with 19th century cast iron street lamps, is a worthy piece of townscape. Many of the little single storey terraces of red-brick houses further up the Grand canal, particularly along the stretch to Harold's Cross bridge,

have a delightful environment; with improvement and rehabilitation these could continue to provide local communities with low-cost city housing of good quality.

Grand Canal Harbour: This area contains several high-quality warehouse and industrial buildings, which, apart from great interest and importance from the point of view of industrial archaeology, are of a high architectural quality. The original layout of the harbour complex had great architectural unity and, although that unity is now fragmented and blurred with unsympathetic building, the high-quality buildings remain. The best of these are the curved warehouse at the round end of the harbour, and the large brick Guinness building; but there are several smaller buildings of competing quality. The whole area deserves a sensitive re-development plan, including an evaluation for conservation and re-use where necessary of the better buildings. The Grand canal as far as Clondalkin has a couple of derelict lock-keepers' houses which date from the construction of the canal.

These are of historic importance and, being small and of simple good design, present no problems for re-building and re-use, perhaps offering an opportunity for a student project or other forms of voluntary labour.

The Royal Canal: This has few if any areas related architecturally to the canal and offers therefore greater possibilities of urban renewal based on the waterway. There are, however, several warehouses and old schools along the city stretches of the canal which offer possibilities for conversion to community use and thereby preserve and continue the special canal-side character. The suburban stretches of the canal contain several excellent examples of victorian cottages, railway buildings, lodges etc., which all contribute to the pleasant environment of the towpath walks, already well used and much appreciated by the local communities. These could all be preserved and improved and become part of the long-term linear park proposals for the Royal canal.

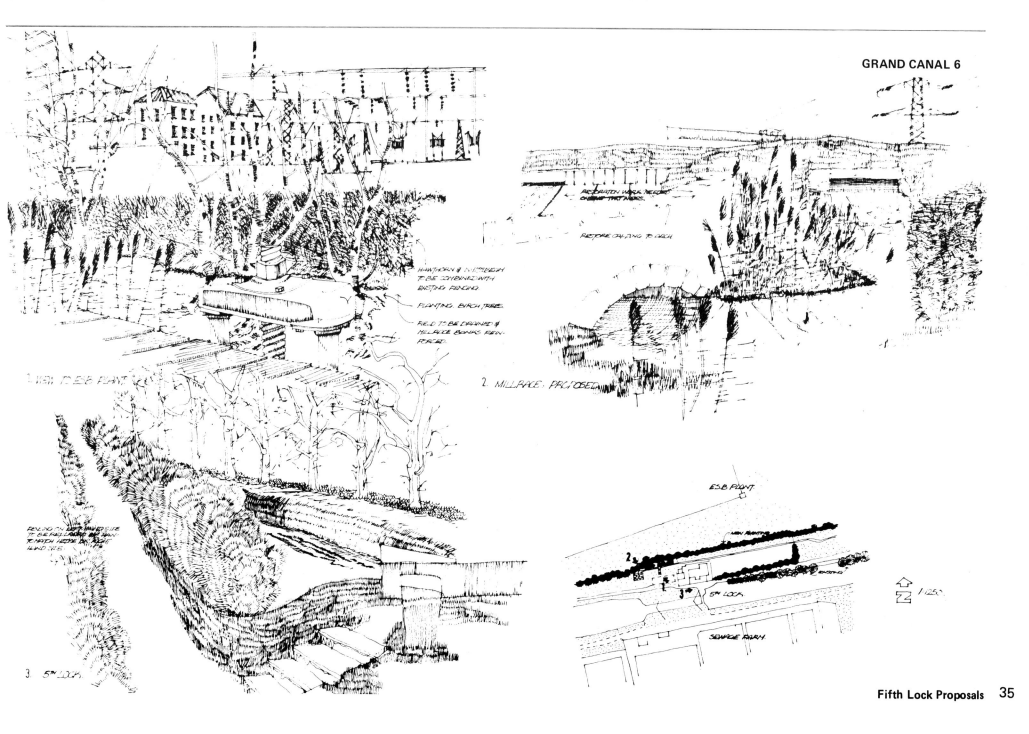

GRAND CANAL 6

Canal Furniture and Details

A remarkable amount of canal furniture and details remain, in various states of repair from excellent to semi-ruinous. These range from lock gates, bollards, metal rings and railings to docks, kerbs, steps, copings, bridges, lettering and paving. All of these, being irreplaceable, need rescue and repair. Many of the stone docks — for instance, along the Grand canal near Baggot street bridge — could be restored and used for seating and recreation. The stone copings, dwarf walls etc. deserve better of our generation than to be patched up in an extremely shoddy manner as has happened in the vicinity of Percy place. The civic pride of the 18th and 19th centuries which built this waterway needs reawakening. The paths and open areas near locks need careful detailing and treatment with hard and soft landscaping to cope with recreational use. The Royal canal in the Spencer dock area has several unique metal lifting bridges which are worth preserving for engineering history; they are also a delight to the eye.

3.5   At least one well-restored canal building

3.6   An echo of Van Gogh

GRAND CANAL 7

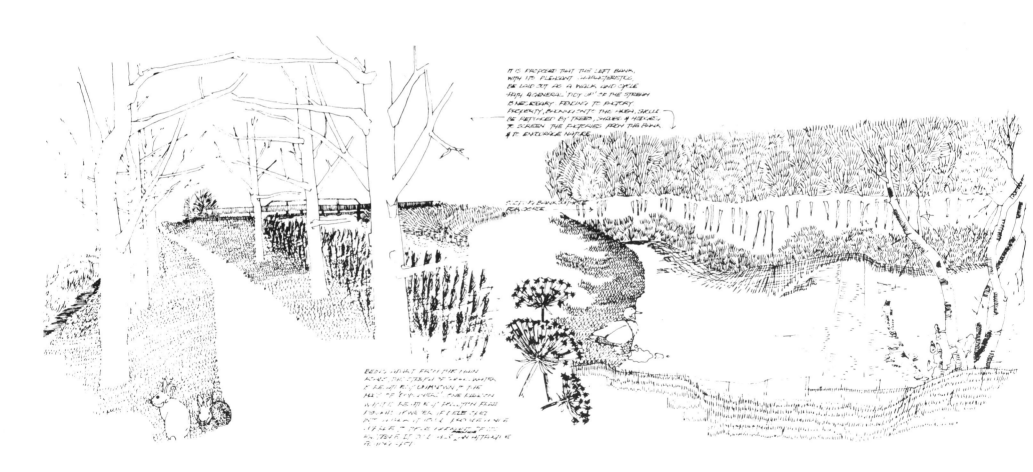

The James' harbour area has some of the finest examples of cobbled floorscape left in Dublin. These are fine by any standards, and should be preserved as examples of Irish craft and design of a high order.

Recreation and Landscaping
Probably the greatest value the two canals offer, and one which should not be lightly despoiled, is that of linear parkways which serve many areas on both sides of the city otherwise deficient in open space. Both canals have towpaths or footpaths open for most of their length and (at least in respect of the Grand canal) open and walkable as far as the river Shannon, over 80 miles away. The possibilities for both active and passive recreation that these two waterways and their banks offer is immense, and as yet only partly realised. Proper reinstatement of the long-distance footpaths along both canals is overdue. The waterways as " living streets " are an attraction to the stroller and local inhabitant. More seats need to be provided on the Grand canal; the Royal has up to now been almost entirely neglected.

For active recreation, boating is the obvious choice, and this can range from inland waterway cruises to canoe-practice by local youth groups. The closed stretch, made safe to James' harbour, would be ideal for this purpose. Safer detailing of the verges and banks, and provision of means of rescue, particularly at locks, is essential to allay the fears of those who invariably see water as a menace to safety.

Landscaping
Both canals should be the subject of an immediate programme of tree planting, combined with the conservation of the existing species. Much new planting of suitable species is required and the co-operation of local groups would help to reduce vandalism. The flat developments from Dolphin's Barn westward would particularly benefit from a large-scale landscaping and tree planting effort, combined with the development of more playgrounds. The stretch of canal along Davitt road needs little except more trees to make it an excellent parkway.

Conclusion
The following quotation from " Italian Townscape " by Ivor de Wolffe sums up much of the fascination that water in towns has for citizens.
" Consider what water has meant to Venice. In the early days of the Republic it defended her from her enemies, later it carried her trade; later still fresh invasions from beyond the Alps and Danube brought the vandals back, water-worshippers by this time, casting gold into her lap for the right to billet their legions in her gondolas. Nature deals the town-planner two perpetual wild cards, water and a hill.
Water's liabilities have a way of becoming its assets. It is iridescent, goes up and down and yet remains flat, charms, hypnotises, invites you in or over by putting the obstacle of itself in the way.
An element which is genuinely elemental, it provides a foil to modern pressures, an antidote to levity in the form of danger, recuperative sounds, elegiac sights. The range of its moods is wider far than those of any other natural phenomenon; hence as an expander of Civilia's emotional compass it is in a class by itself ".

GRAND CANAL 8

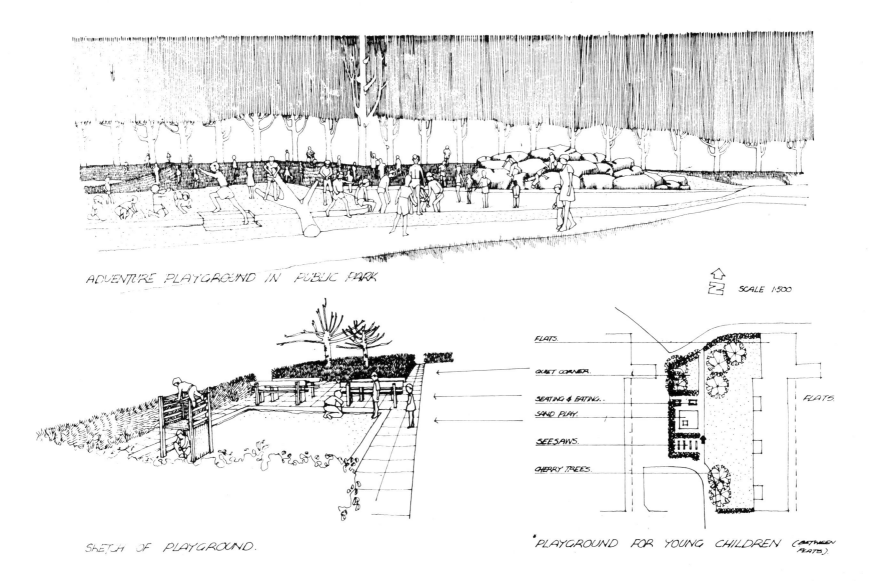

ADVENTURE PLAYGROUND IN PUBLIC PARK

SCALE 1:500

SKETCH OF PLAYGROUND.

FLATS.

QUIET CORNER.

SEATING & EATING..

SAND PLAY.

SEESAWS.

CHERRY TREES.

FLATS.

*PLAYGROUND FOR YOUNG CHILDREN (BETWEEN FLATS).

The Inner City

Street Infill:
The Centre
by Robin Walker
and
Stephen Woulfe Flanagan

Infill Policy
in
Existing Streets
by Peter D'Arcy

Reproduction:
For and Against
by Francis Barry

Streets
Streetscapes
and Traffic
by John Costello

City Housing Improvement
by Shane de Blacam
and Loughlin Kealy

City Housing
Redevelopment
by James Pike

Space About Buildings
by Andrew Devane

Street Infill: The Centre

by Robin Walker
and
Stephen Woulfe Flanagan

Communities basically are the same everywhere. They enjoy a common hierarchy of functions which give expression to their existence; and whilst the functions and size of community may vary, there exists an order within any community which makes areas within it comprehensible and identifiable. This factor we understand by 'Character'.

Character is an element by which individuals within a community can sustain themselves because it both stems from, and generates, a sense of belonging to *their* city, *their* area, *their* street. It is also an element that can be created, maintained or destroyed by architectural decision. In discussing the question of 'Infill' in any city situation, we are talking about city character — its retention, its renewal or its change. It is therefore important to understand the factors which establish this quality of character (be it good or bad) in a particular area if we are to act responsibly and meaningfully, in a situation where we are required to 'Infill'.

Character, in this context, is the intangible quality which is the result of people in community giving concrete visual expression to their daily existence, i.e. the enclosing of a hierarchy of functions. The concrete expression of this enclosure is in the fabric of the city — the assembly of appreciable units which, when put together establish the urban walls and floors. "The outside of the building is the inside of the town".

Character is, therefore, the product of

1. PEOPLE—Their superficial characteristics change more rapidly in this century than ever before: their basic human virtues, failings and needs alter slowly, if at all.
2. USE —including function.
3. FABRIC—the appreciable units of enclosure, their material, size and relationship.

The architectural character of Dublin in general derives from the architecture of many centuries; that of the centre derives principally from the predominance of its 18th century buildings and the 18th century street pattern. It comes from the simple gridiron planning of streets and squares and from the simplistic geometric or more accurately arithmetic composition of the dead-pan plain thin facades of houses and minor buildings. The houses of Henrietta street and the old library in Trinity College show clearly how it lies in the stream from Palladio to Mies van der Rohe rather than that from Michaelangelo to Le Corbusier; and its roots, as with the art of all periods in Ireland, are still deeper, buried firmly in the linear open-ended culture of north western Europe rather than in the centric closed culture of the Mediterranean.

Underlying the superficial similarities of materials and techniques and overriding the superficial differences in the styles of the 18th and 19th centuries, it is this root fibre running through all historic periods up to the present century that has created the harmonious and distinctive character of Dublin's centre.

There are many examples of streets in Dublin which by infilling have, in the past, changed their fabric, the scale of their fabric and, therefore their character. Lord Edward street is one which has replaced mediaeval, and later georgian, dwelling houses mixed with small offices, by much larger scale buildings for purely office use. Has the street lost in character or gained in character? It certainly epitomises the bureaucratic aspects of our period. Another example is O'Connell street where change of use and fabric has altered its character from a predominantly residential street with small shops to a honky-tonk mix of large banks, department stores, seedy cafes and so on, exhibiting a huge variety of scale and style. This, the main thoroughfare of our capital city, has lost its character and style; the result is featureless, insipid, even hideous.

St. Stephen's green appears to have been continuously in a state of flux, and in renewing its fabric it has generally increased the size of its individual buildings. Who can doubt that it has lost its 18th century character; its 19th century character, which was different; and will lose its very different 20th century character. So what?

Perhaps the best example of all is Dame street which, without changing its essential use, has changed the style and scale of its fabric and most certainly has changed its character. For the worse?

Perhaps the historical lesson to be learned is that change must be gradual to be unnoticeable. And that for it to be unnoticeable is what people, living in this period of traumatic change, seem to desire. To be unnoticeable, change must take place over as long a period as possible and in as small increments as possible. Neither of these requirements is an architectural problem. When, however, as has recently happened, renewal and change take place at a rapid pace, and where the size of new buildings is required by their use to be considerably bigger than the existing buildings, it is sometimes felt that some architectural palliative exists which can be applied to make this change less noticeable. This is not the case. Such a palliative could not be described as architectural in the full sense of that term. Unless, therefore, we are prepared to allow Dublin to degenerate architecturally and lose what architectural distinction from the past it has, (a distinction founded in the reasonableness both structural and functional with which buildings in the past answered the needs of their period) we must either accept that the consequence of change and renewal will be change in character, or else develop ways and incentives to limit the nature of the change and the consequent need for renewal. This also is not an architectural problem.

If, however, means can be found for limiting the degree of change required by confining the use and limiting the size of new developments, then the success of infilling and gradual change in character of the environment *does* become an architectural problem.

Despite the capacity of towns and cities for change, they sometimes need support for conservation not only of fabric but also of use. Clearly a balance has to be struck between capacity and need; and one aspect of this balance could be the level of public subsidy available. For too long we have assumed that conservation required only subsidy in the form of grants for the repair of buildings or environmental improvement. There may well prove to be a need for a broader social subsidy from central Government, in order to achieve conservation in a socially acceptable way. Additional subsidy is required to support and stimulate central city housing and stimulate work opportunity which may suffer from a restriction on growth.

We have seen that the element of character relies on three major factors, People, Use and Fabric; and how these three factors have been responsible for changing the environment of Dublin. We have also seen that it may be in the interest of the city to limit the nature of the change and the consequent need for renewal.

In the context of street infill in the city centre it is essential to distinguish areas which can and should be conserved; areas where gradual renewal and change may take place; and areas to be totally redeveloped. In this way we would have a hierarchy of development which would give us some directives as to the extent of change and what would be significant in terms of these changes for the existing character. Such areas could be defined as follows:

1. AREAS FOR TOTAL CONSERVATION — that is, areas where it is intended to retain both Use and the Fabric. The product of this will come closest to the retention of Character. The retention of character cannot, however, be complete because People, the third factor, is constantly changing. For example, an area of 19th century housing occupied by 19th century people is obviously going to be different in character from 19th century housing occupied by 20th century people. Into this category the finest areas of 18th century Dublin, Fitzwilliam square, Merrion square etc. clearly fall. The use has changed, but not beyond the stage of making a reversal possible.

2. AREAS FOR CONSERVATION OF FABRIC — that is, areas where it is intended to retain the Fabric whilst making efforts to adopt new Uses within it for new People. Whilst retaining the fabric, it is unlikely that, if one changes the use, one will in fact retain the character. Evidence of this is clearly shown in Merrion and Fitzwilliam squares, primarily from the desertion of the squares by families and the incursion by the professions. The absence of children and prams, the saturation of the streets with motor cars, and the forest of name-plates on every door are merely superficial symptoms of the very radical change in character which has overtaken the area; and whilst the architectural character has not so noticeably changed, the fact of the new ESB offices points to what might ultimately happen if control of use is not considered as an aspect of the successful retention of fabric. Into this category fall such areas as Leeson street and Lower Baggot street.

3. AREAS FOR RETENTION OF USE AND RENEWAL OF FABRIC — that is, areas where it is intended to retain the Use as far as is possible whilst renewing the Fabric. This entails infilling gradually with new buildings. Here again however if the uses of the new buildings are different as well as the fabric, the character will change.

For example, if one were to infill with a new building in a family housing area and retain the Use as family housing, the character-change would not be as great as if one were to vary the use to single-person accommodation. But nevertheless if the environment changes and the Use does not, there will also be a character change. For example if the roadway itself in Moore street retained its Use-characteristic for street trading but the use and fabric of the buildings which frame it changed from small shops to large department stores, it would immediately lose its present character. Dame street, O'Connell street, Grafton street, Henry street and others fall also into this category.

4. AREAS FOR TOTAL CHANGE — that is, areas where it is intended to change the Use *and* the

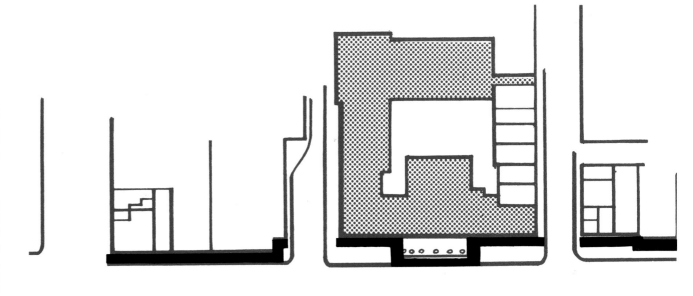

O'CONNELL STREET

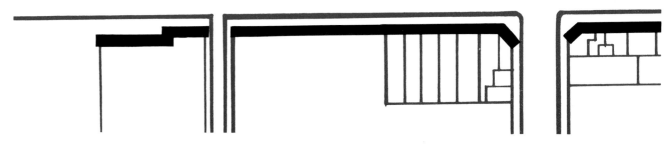

4.2 *Bold projecting portico dominates the street*

40

Fabric. This will create a new Character. Whilst these areas, and areas 1 and 2, are outside the brief of 'Street Infill' they illustrate the essential part played by Use and Fabric in generating character. Streets such as Abbey street may fall into this category even if change of use might not be total. This last category is also felt to be outside the scope of this paper because in such areas rapid and radical change would be acceptable, and therefore the concept of 'Infill' does not apply.

Fabric and Use

If means can be found to limit the contrast in the proposed new use with the existing in terms of size and kind, then the architectural problem of Infill becomes manageable. This is especially true of centre city areas where we are considering replacement of the fabric – that is, category 3 above.

Historically, Dublin is formed of areas which are concerned with small scale use and small scale fabric. There are some exceptions, as in the case of large public buildings, churches etc. which have been specially handled so that they can take their place in the small fabric. In a modern context this is still the problem central to Infill, namely, how to adapt large-scale use and physical bulk into an existing small-scale use and unit. Broadly speaking, one can say that the larger the size of the new unit of fabric to be incorporated into the existing environment, the more important its siting becomes. The extent to which the architect can influence such decisions is limited by the degree to which the profession is consulted by its clients, before site acquisition and afterwards.

Typical of these large-scale use-and-unit buildings are the office block and the department store. They represent respectively the short-span tall building and the long-span low building, both of which have become common elements of the city in this century. The department store has some precedent in the late 19th century Big Shop; for example, Todd Burns' building in Henry street. The Big Shop, as in that case, was often located on a corner site, which can take a larger building and stronger treatment than the street in general. In this way, and because of the variation in their storey heights (a characteristic of all the small buildings of the past, relying as they did on the staircase for vertical circulation) the big shops fitted into the urban fabric without destroying it. But whilst the use has not changed essentially, the greater size of the modern department store or shopping centre, and the advent of the lift and escalator which have tended to iron out variations of storey height have, with this type of building, created a new problem for the centre city.

The lift has also been responsible for giving us the modern form of office block in which we no longer have a variety of functions expressed in a hierarchical manner as in the varying storey heights of older buildings, but a series of equal functions expressed as a series of equal storey heights, the only vertical variety being at the ground floor and sometimes top floor where the functions are normally different. A similar building form has been developed for housing in the typical block of flats, which again provides no functional basis for vertical variety. Unless deliberately restricted, both the office block and the flat block tend towards being high buildings.

These new building types, the short span tall building and long span low building, pose, because of their large

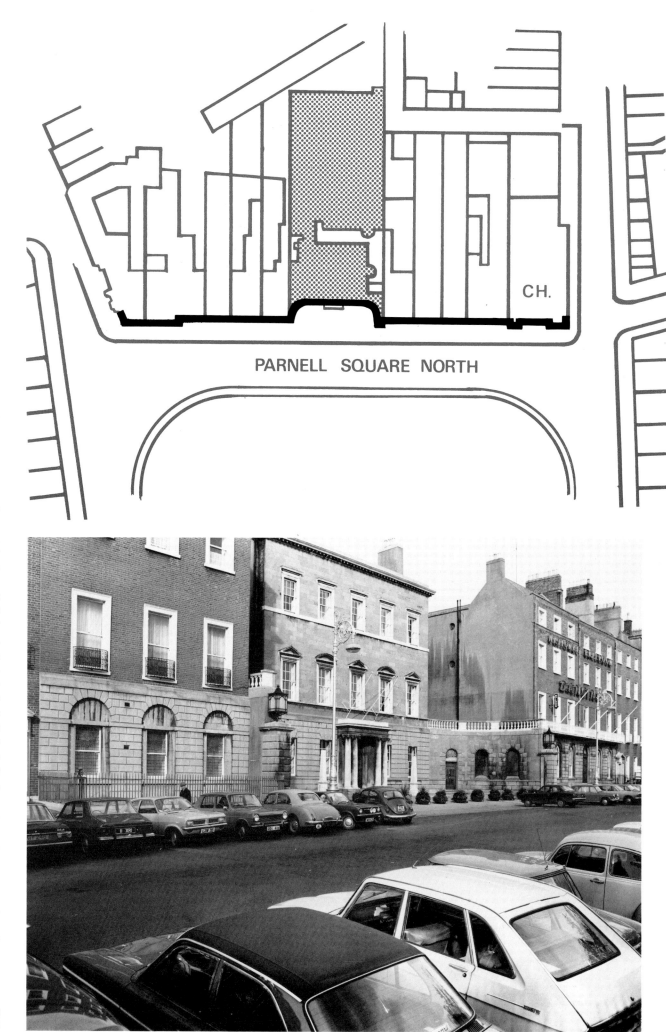

4.5 Subtle incurve dominates by withdrawal

scale use and size, the problem of integration into the small scale use and small fabric structure of the centre.

Past Precedents

A study of some precedents in the past of solutions to this problem in terms of siting may suggest solutions which would be valid in a modern context.

For this study, we have chosen three major buildings of large scale use and large scale function:

1. The G.P.O., O'Connell street
2. Charlemont House (The Municipal Gallery). Parnell square
3. The Royal College of Surgeons, St. Stephen's green

In looking at these three buildings and their street relationships, the most noticeable fact is that they do not in any way try to adopt the street characteristic or be a simple element of it; but whilst they dominate or attempt to dominate the street or square they do not disrupt. By various architectural means they more or less successfully make the transition from small to large scale.

1. The G.P.O., O'Connell street — Here the building has been sited in mid street and has been pulled *forward* off the street building line and allowed to dominate O'Connell street. Its role as the dominant was probably clearer when Nelson's Pillar, which was such a strong visual element, was in the centre of the street. Now since the removal of the Pillar, the G.P.O. must compete with Clerys department store and the Gresham Hotel. Both these buildings are late comers to the scene and are in fact out of scale with the simple elements of the street.

2. CHARLEMONT HOUSE, Parnell square — Again a building which does not attempt to integrate itself into the street characteristic and which is sited *back* from the street building line. It dominates the square by being sited centrally along its side, even though Findlater's church, sited on the street line and on the corner, is a taller building.

3. THE ROYAL COLLEGE OF SURGEONS, St. Stephen's green — Here again is a building of large fabric dominating the west side of St. Stephen's green. It is sited *on plane* with the other buildings of the street and is less successful in acting as a dominant because it does not visually disassociate itself enough from the surrounding fabric.

From these three examples we can see how Dublin in the past has managed to integrate large fabric/large use buildings into a small fabric/small use structure.

This is done by:
1. Not adopting the street characteristic;
2. Allowing the building adopt a dominant role by siting it (a) FORWARD. (b) BACK, (c) ON PLANE.

The placing of a large building back from the street face has many precedents in early modern architecture and can offer a solution for siting one-off buildings of large bulk. The important factor is that of height. This must be very carefully controlled, depending on the type of function the building has and the way in which it can dominate a particular street or area. A department store will usually require large and deep floor spaces, the consequence of which is low bulk. It must be

4.6   Dominance derives from surface modelling

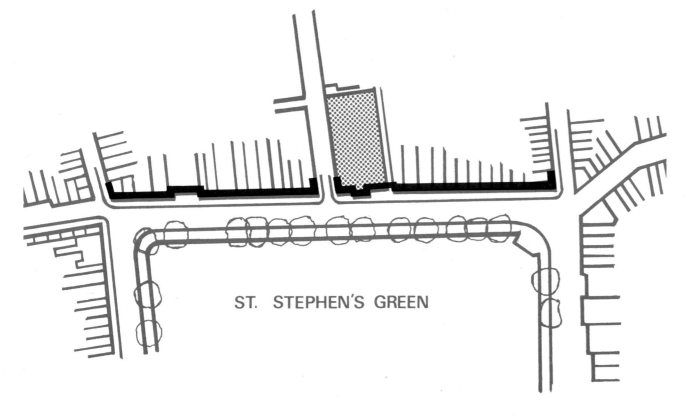

ST. STEPHEN'S GREEN

kept low, and may be allowed to dominate a street by the creation of a piazza, being itself set well back from the street front. An office block may present a similar problem of height and bulk. It will usually require fairly short-span spaces, and may be designed so that verticality is the dominant, rather than horizontality as in the case of the department store. As in the case of the horizontal structure, its verticality can be used as a dominant in the street. In certain circumstances, depending on the part of the city and its functions, the centre area can accept this solution for large buildings; but it is notable that the solution was, in the past, applied in a limited number of cases and it can only be applied occasionally.

These strictly are thoughts on urban design, not architecture, but they offer possible directives in the siting and shaping of major commercial buildings in the centre city area. An architectural solution, which matches that of the best of previous traditional systems, as a result of its reasoned choice of materials and techniques while attempting no superficial imitation of or "harmonisation" with those traditions, will be the solution most likely to maintain the distinguished architectural character of the city. Provided always that a genuine architectural skill is devoted to the new work — for quality and distinction do not lie exclusively in materials and techniques — and provided also, that what constitutes the architectural character of Dublin as already described, is understood.

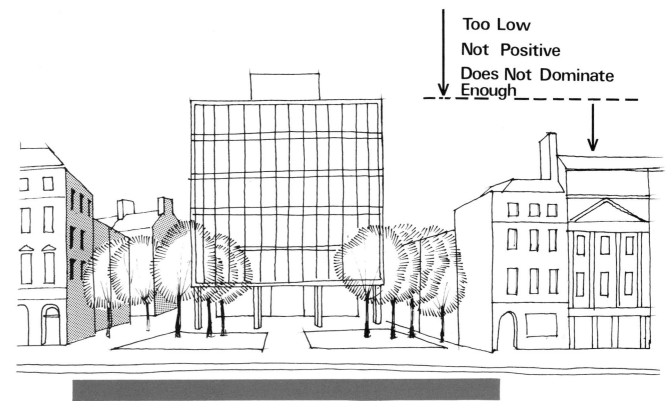

Too Low
Not Positive
Does Not Dominate Enough

4.9   Half-hearted statement is unconvincing

Replacing the Fabric

The problem of inserting large developments into the centre might be solved in the ways suggested above; there remains the problem of rebuilding, in smaller units, the basic fabric of the centre. Earlier in this paper it was suggested that, if means can be found to limit the contrast in size and kind of the new with the existing fabric, then the architectural problem becomes manageable. In particular, if the module of unit width in the street and the typical variation in storey heights can be maintained, the problem is greatly simplified.

It remains, however, a problem. It is implicit in the idea of infill that change is inevitable (otherwise it would be logical to attempt to reproduce the existing buildings) and one must therefore accept that variety

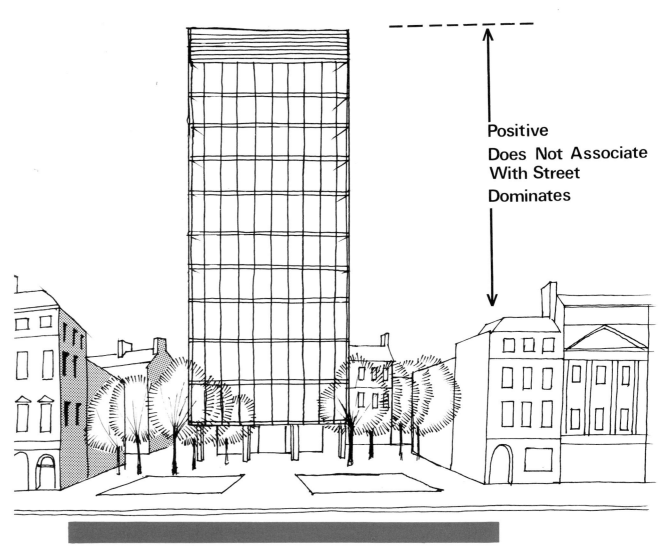

Positive
Does Not Associate With Street
Dominates

4.8   *Charlemont House and Findlater's Church*

4.10   *Bold statement is more acceptable*

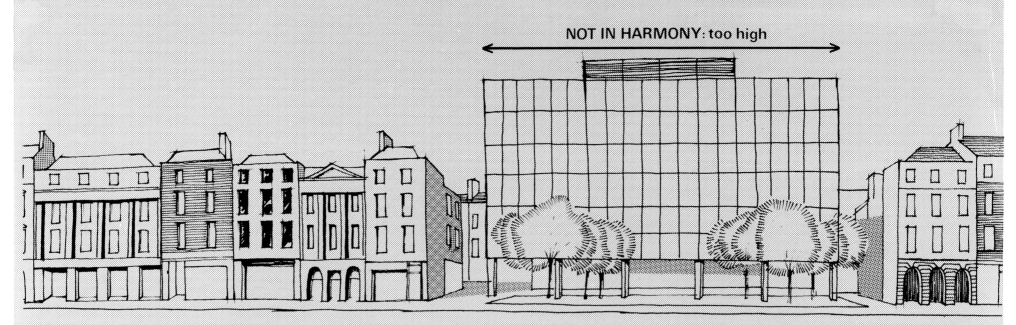

NOT IN HARMONY: too high

4.11 Because of breadth, height becomes oppressive

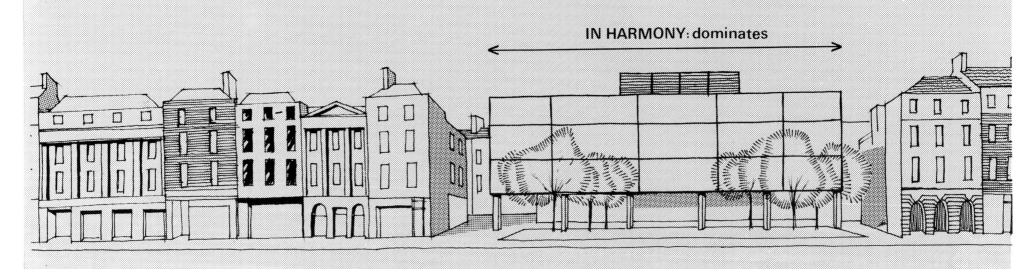

IN HARMONY: dominates

4.12 Dominant in scale and yet harmonious

4.13 Sequential Infill: One

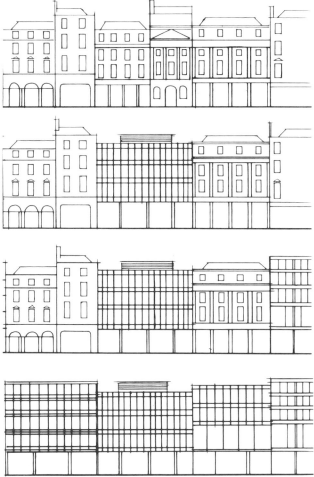

4.14 Sequential Infill: Two

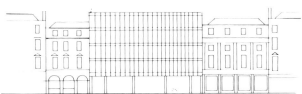

4.15 Sequential Infill: Three

at least, if not contrast (or indeed dissonance) will be the result. It is the acceptable degree of variety and speed of change which will determine the nature of the architectural solution and its success. Judgement on this can be derived only from each particular situation, from the particular environment and from the size of the proposed infill. The judgement should be left, ideally, to those most intimately concerned — that is, the client and users, the architect and the local people, in that order. Only in cases of conflict should the central authority become involved. This suggests that a devolution of central authority power might be desirable. In arriving at that judgement, however, there is one general guiding principle underlying the question of degree; and that principle derives from the understanding of the architectural character of the city. If Dublin has in general a distinctive architectural character it does not result from a superficial similarity in its buildings, but from an essential fibre running through the art of all its periods. Whether the buildings of the city are in brick, stone, steel or concrete, it is the understanding and expression of this essential fibre that will maintain harmony and ensure the retention for the future of the established architectural character of Dublin.

Infill Policy in Existing Streets

by Peter D'Arcy

Dublin city, long a European backwater, is now coming under increasing pressures for development—pressures which have already caused so much damage to other cities more advanced than our own. The aim of this study is to promote a greater awareness of our existing environment, isolating and recognising the features which make our city attractive so that we can channel and direct new development into courses which recognise and contribute to the essential qualities of Dublin.

Scope

This study attempts to define infill architecture in its various forms, and to relate these to the city and its street patterns. It aims to show that, while size is a major factor in any form of infill, principles can be established which offer positive guidelines and allow conflicts between form and function to be resolved. It then catalogues parts of the existing architectural 'vocabulary' of the city and relates these to some of the new developments taking place in the city.

Wider Relevance

The study concerns itself with Dublin only, although the main points it makes will hopefully have a relevance in urban situations throughout the country. It in fact concentrates on the area within the two canals, and its relevance outside this area will derive from the criteria and principles evolved rather than from any details illustrated.

All architecture involves infilling; the differences lie in the degree of infill. For present purposes infill architecture means ' any new building inserted in an existing built environment, especially an environment with such strong characteristics that it must impose some of these characteristics on any new building '. This definition by its very broadness covers all the situations in which infill architecture will arise. It can be seen that the degree of infill required in any situation must be a direct response to the strength of existing characteristics and forms. Four main categories of infill situation arise:

A) (e.g. Merrion square) where the character is so strong and the building forms are so consistent

Infill in existing streets can create problems of scale

and unified that it is necessary to consider matching the existing buildings precisely—by *reproduction*.

B) (e.g. Stephen's green, north) where the character is strong but the forms of buildings are not as consistent or as unified as in (a) above; in this case a new building could vary from the buildings around it but would conform to their strongest characteristics, perhaps in colour or texture or in height or in window treatment.

C) (e.g. O'Connell street) where the character of an area depends less on similarities between buildings but more on their differences of style or idiom, and where the main characteristics in common are those of scale, building line or height.

D) (e.g. Burlington road) where the buildings are detached from one another, separated and screened by mature trees, and where conditions of height and building line are common. In a case such as this, any building would be termed infill in the loosest sense only and could vary within very broad limits before it would damage the overall area provided that the landscaping and site treatment match that of the locality.

Streets
In an historic urban area the strongest characteristic of the environment is *the street*. The maintenance of the form and character of streets and streetscapes is the basic rationale of infill architecture. There are two main types of street: the cartesian corridor street, having one building line, a constant height (with small variations on occasion) with buildings depending on one another visually and often structurally; and the more organic or 'natural' street or avenue where both building line and height are haphazard and where the buildings are often detached from one another. The buildings in a corridor street are almost always two-sided (front and back) and thus usually fall into infill categories A, B or C above. The buildings in an avenue are often four-sided and as such fit into category D above.

The prime consideration in relation to infill architecture is therefore that any new building should be conscious of and respond to its surroundings; in the words of the late Tristan Edwards, "maintaining an attitude of good manners towards its neighbours."

Environment
Infill begins with a closely observed study of the existing environment, listing the main characteristics of the locality and assessing these in order of importance. The character of Dublin results from its characteristic scale, texture and colour, the relationship of solid to void in its street walls, its use of detail, all within the tight frame and pattern of its corridor streets.

Scale
There are two forms of scale: vertical and horizontal. The vertical scale in Dublin arises from the four-storey georgian house, with its decrease in window size and its use of many devices to stress the ground and first floor levels. The horizontal unit of scale derives from the georgian plot width of between 7.5 and 9 metres (25-30 feet). The difficulty of matching the unitary nature of the existing streetscape has been the main stumbling-block to successful infill architecture in Dublin—the problem of replacing small

residential units, now used as offices, with large office units.

Texture
Most new buildings now attempt to conform in texture and colour with the buildings around them. The brick is the unit in most areas of Dublin and it is now being used quite freely. It provides the variation in colour and texture that is so much a part of most Dublin vistas.

External Walls
As can be seen from some of the illustrations below, the relationship of solid to void (or window to external wall) changed in Dublin during the speculative office building boom of the nineteen-sixties. However, the energy crisis coupled with increasing sophistication in office space-utilisation has recently led to a return to smaller windows, resulting in buildings with more affinity to their surroundings.

Functional Scale
However, *scale* in Dublin does not just mean physical

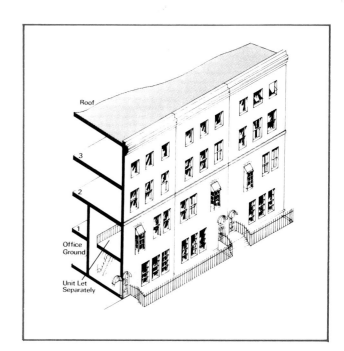

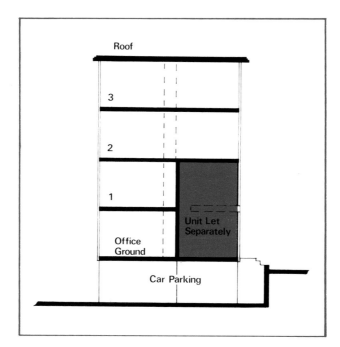

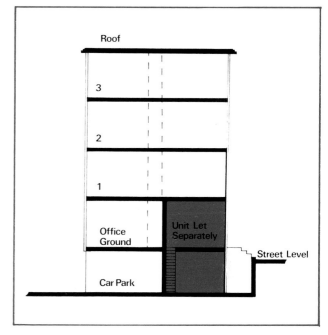

METHOD 1 *(see p. 48)*

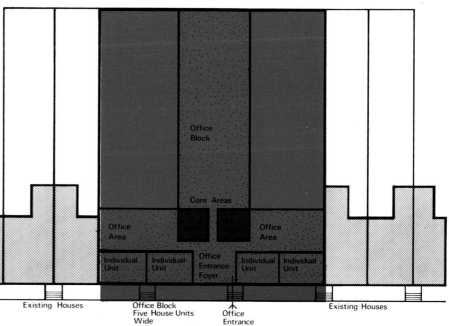

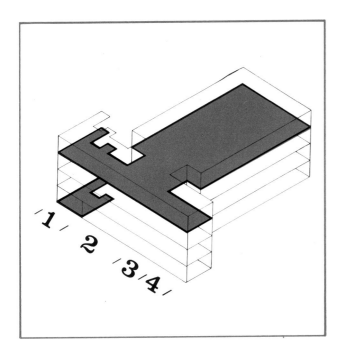

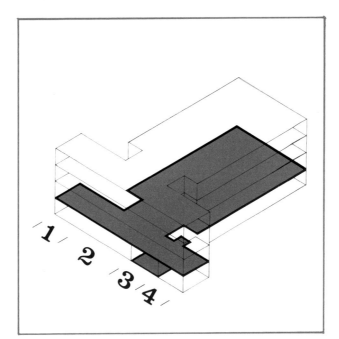

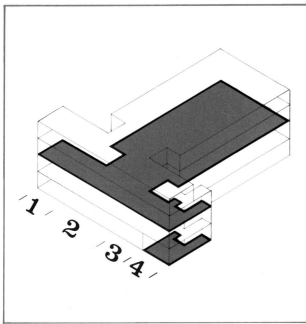

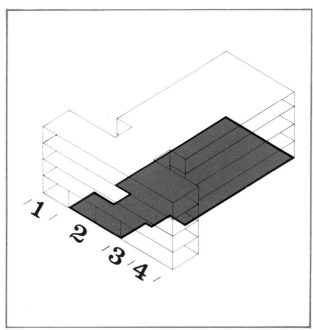

scale. There existed in Dublin in the past a proliferation of small scale businesses, offices and workshops. Rapid industrialisation and the growth of bureaucracy led to an increase in the demand for large units of office space; this led to a change in functional scale. Where before two house units were replaced with one office block, now as often as not six or seven house units are replaced by a single office block.

Size

However, it will be seen from the definition of infill architecture above that the city must be seen as an entity and therefore that even a large building (even one replacing an entire terrace) is still an infill building and should be designed as such. Infill architecture is a matter of environment and not of isolated streetscapes.

This being so it is necessary to devise some methods of breaking up and reducing the scale of large office units.

Method 1

48 Two methods are illustrated. The first provides space

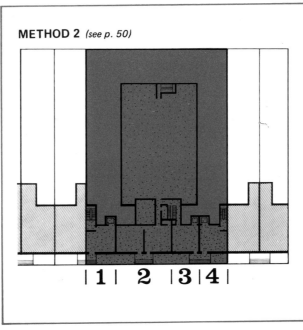

METHOD 2 *(see p. 50)*

|1| 2 |3|4|

METHOD 2 *(see p. 50)*

for a collection of small-scale uses at the front of any building of more than three city modules (three house units wide). These units would each be the width of one house plot and would have independent access. They would have a depth of four to five metres; they could be one or two storeys over basement. In the case of two-storey units, they would occupy the ground floor and the basement or first floor. Single-storey units would occupy the ground floor only. These units could be used as residential units or could be let independently for small-scale business uses (doctors, solicitors, architects, etc.).

Zoning

To make this proposal attractive to a developer it would be necessary for the Corporation to allow such units to be built in addition to the maximum permitted plot ratio for the site. All that this would involve would be the creation of a new zoning similar to the existing General Business zone. However, this zoning should be much more flexible, so that the

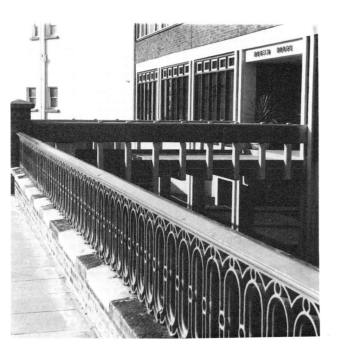

Residential Buildings

The problems of scale associated with large-scale office development do not arise with residential development, since residential functions are varied yet determinate, as opposed to speculative office development where the functions are predictable but occupancy is by definition indeterminate.

It is important to stress this role of buildings as units in an overall streetscape. Infill buildings should be judged on their contribution to the street as a grouping rather than on their own individual qualities. It may happen in certain circumstances that a building would improve or point up a streetscape by breaking the height line or the building line. The revisions due to the Dublin development plan should include a city-wide streetscape analysis which would locate such points and would classify the areas of the city on their environmental values and potentials rather than just on their uses; elsewhere, departures from established height, scale or pattern should be handled sensitively and with caution.

mixture of uses will be fostered as described, rather than hindered.

Method 2

This involves letting any large office building on a floor by floor basis. However, each floor has an independent entrance hall at ground floor level, with independent access to that floor. The only additional expense in this case would be the cost of an additional lift. This method offers flexibility in letting as the floors may be let either independently or in various combinations.

The Eye Level

The rationale of both the above methods is that the scale of the city registers primarily at ground level and that any detail at this level is of prime importance to the maintenance of the original small scale. Both these methods attempt to keep small-scale units at street level.

Illustrations

The photographs relate a series of traditional details in the city to their modern equivalents. They fall into the following categories:

- Entrances
- Windows
- Facades
- Parapets
- Roofscape/chimneys
- Plinths
- Areas
- General

Reproduction: For and Against

by Francis Barry

SECTION 1: RESTORATION

This paper relates to buildings in Dublin built between 1750 and 1900 and generally to terraced houses in corridor streets or in squares. Individual buildings of outstanding merit are, it is hoped, already protected by listing and ownership by the state or by the good, e.g. Powerscourt house, south William street, or Belvedere house; but beware what happened in the extensions to the latter!

Problems and Responsibilities

Owners of buildings are temporary custodians for posterity; the theoretically absolute rights of private property conferred by the constitution are constrained by legislation and do not give the 'owner' the 'right' to deface, demolish or rebuild without very good reason.

All living things suffer a cycle of birth, maturity, decay and final demise.

" As man, perhaps the moment of his breath,
   Receives the lurking principle of death,
   The young disease, which must subdue at length,
   Grows with his growth and strengthens with his
   strength."

(Alexander Pope on Man).

Over a longer time-span, the same fate overtakes the man-made. A building starts decaying from the moment of its completion and requires continuous maintenance, repair and, sooner or later, replacement.

6.1   Streetscape restored: 89, 90, 91 and 92 Lower Leeson Street

Buildings modulate and decay because of their enemies —

Age: climate acting on finite building materials (in Ireland, perhaps more rapidly than in most places);

Accident (or Acts of Architects): collapse after construction due to inadequate or over-daring structural design (Beauvais cathedral is the extreme example) or settlement of subsoil;

collapse due to timber decay, particularly dry and wet rot (one recalls the crisis period of collapses in Dublin about a decade ago);

Acts of God: fire, tempest, flood, earthquake;

Acts of Man: motor vehicles vibrating the fabric or (rarely) colliding with it;

road widening to hasten traffic flow;

the neglect of poverty and (a new nastiness) purposeful neglect for gain;

demolishing for whim, profit or dislike of ancestors;

altering for self-aggrandisement (late victorian ironwork and porches);

war and civil unrest, bombing (Belfast, Merrion square embassy);

profit motive — the needless greed of an unscrupulous developer.

Changes of Use
The vertical circulation of georgian and victorian houses and their (domestic) usage, naturally depended on social and economic factors. They were designed for the relatively rich minority, in single occupancy, and depended for the functioning on a small army of servants. Steadily since the Act of Union in 1800, houses have decayed and many are gone (Gardiner street) or defaced (plastered facades). Some, particularly those owned by some religious orders, have always been well maintained; others more recently in times of property boom have justified to developer-owners the cost of extensive refurbishing. Now in times of recession our stock, while enjoying a temporary respite from greed, is in greater peril from neglect.

Given goodwill and money, very few of the existing houses are incapable of being sanely restored, without extreme quasi-archaeological finesse, and re-used as dwellings, for at least another hundred years. Alas, many, basically sound, have been destroyed for dubious reasons and, sadly, some architects — at the best through misguided barbarism, at the worst, merely for gain — have connived at that destruction.

Generally it is assumed that a building's physical meaning consists of the *sum of its parts*: it visual surfaces (externally and internally), its plan form, its fabric and its details. The total retention of these is often impossible; the problem arises however where this possibility does exist but is in conflict with renewal, economics or adaption to use. In these cases the assessment of value is an essential guide to forming a valid approach to the aesthetic, technical or economic problem.

Reinstatement Proposals
I: The (purist) Ideal
To take an 18th or 19th century terrace house, intact and in reasonable repair and fully restore facade and area, interior, original returns, rear, roofs, garden and mews, so as to appear on completion as nearly as possible as it did when originally built, taking particular care to preserve, to the greatest extent practicable, the patina of age. Most important of all, to use it subsequently as a dwelling in single occupancy.

The facade should have all later excrescences removed, any large-pane windows and plain fansashes being replaced with replicas of the traditional barred sash; insensitive 'cleaning' of brickwork or stonework should be avoided and if re-pointing must be done it is of paramount importance to use expert bricklayers. Front door ironmongery and incongruous letterboxes should be replaced with ones matching the originals, as should railings, gates, steps, pavings and basement entrances.

The interior should likewise be fully restored by removing all later partitioning, restoring and repairing joinery, plasterwork (including decorative work where this is fit for salvage), ironmongery, fireplaces (preferably with secondhand originals where obtainable).

All existing layers of wallpaper and of paint should be stripped and colours for redecoration should be chosen from the classical palette. Services present the greatest problems; only the eccentric would still wish to use candles or oil for lighting, open coal fires throughout for heating, privy or chamber-pot for sanitary accommodation or a well for cold water supply. Some compromise is obviously necessary; but the results should be as unobtrusive as possible.

Earlier compromise has produced on most backs layers or additions which should be removed, where these are incongruous in style or unduly bulky. In many cases, especially in exposed locations, rear walls have been rendered. These can only be retained or renewed, since stripping down is not only prohibitive in cost but would not produce the desired result. Paint or stucco may prove the answer. Roofs will need repair or renewal, as will granite copings, leadwork, slating, chimney stacks. Mews buildings should be restored (since coaches, horses and hawks are normally no longer kept in town) altered to dwelling perhaps only on upper floor, but held to the original building line, not set back to widen the lanes as the Corporation now seeks to do. The motorcar, if admitted at all, should be confined to the former coach house and not allowed in to the open garden. Gardens should be retained as gardens. Some hard surfaces may be acceptable if properly landscaped; but greenery should predominate and the motorcar be rigorously excluded.

24 Fitzwilliam square (c. 1820) is an almost ideal example of the purist approach. The latest built are untypical, because of their comparative youth and construction and are generally in sound condition. The two-hundred-year-old houses on the north side, many of which have been used as tenements for more than half their lives (e.g. north Great George's street), are a quite different and more difficult problem; but even in the Gardiner estate some splendid restorations have been carried out, especially in Mountjoy square.

II: The Necessary Compromise
To replace, in a streetscape, a single or at the most two units, destroyed completely or partially by accident, neglect or active vandalism. The reproduction in near-replica of the facades of the British Embassy in Merrion square is an obvious example, although here the (presumed) continued partial use of the building as offices will pose other problems.

III. The Acceptable Compromise 1
To attempt to restore, as in I above and use as a dwelling for the single residential occupancy of a community or the like. Numbers 89, 90, 91 and 92 lower Leeson street were partially restored for the Society of Mary to act as a community house for the priests of the Catholic University School.

Financial restrictions precluded the complete replacement of the window bars on the facades in earlier alterations, particularly to the facade of number 89, and the doors in party walls could not be jettisoned. Also, provision of new services resulted in inevitable damage to the integrity of the original fabric. However, the main rooms were nearly all restored, and a splendid ceiling was uncovered and repaired in the music room.

IV: The Acceptable Compromise 2
To attempt to restore as in I above but for use as dwellings, preferably a maximum of five flats, one to each floor.

This use had of course occupied the majority of houses (other than 'tenements') in the central area until office use became more profitable. It nearly always resulted in the fragmentation of the internal cells and the partial defacement of the rear. The services problem, however carefully considered, would naturally be five-fold, particularly in the provision of external pipe stacks.

A 'community' use by bachelors or families, with shared minimum services, could reduce defacement of the outside of the building.

V: The Almost Acceptable Compromise
Partially to restore and use other than for dwelling, in whole or in part. Assuming that owners comply with the provisions of the Housing Act 1969, and can obtain permission for a change to non-residential use, this would seem to provide the greatest chance for the survival of the major part of present surviving stock by using the buildings as offices, which would make the spending of the necessary sums an economic proposition.

Unfortunately, the demands of modern office standards and the requirements of the building by-laws generally result in drastic internal alterations, particularly if a lift is installed and an alternative means of escape from the upper floors is required. Although this solution normally keeps the facades intact and therefore the streetscape, and is beloved of the preservation-

6.2   *Frontal pastiche with unrelated return building (1975)*

6.3   *Proposed rebuilding of a streetscape: 2, 3 and 4 Ely Place*

6.4   *Facade restored: 24 Fitzwilliam Square*

ist romantics, the destruction of the backlands becomes almost total — the gardens cruelly paved for car-parking, the mews demolished. Various additions are also usually built onto the rear, to house liftshafts and lavatories.

Bad Example: Grand House in Merrion square with low-cost modern office block occupying as much of the area of the garden as the architect has persuaded Dublin Corporation to allow.

SECTION 2 — REPRODUCTION
The Concise Oxford Dictionary 1964 gives the following definitions:
   REPLICA: " Duplicate made *by original artist* of his picture etc; facsimile, exact copy ".
   PASTICHE (PASTICCIO): " Medley made up from various sources composed in the style of *a known author*". (Italics mine.   F.B.)

Reproduction: Replica 1
Apart from necessary compromise, as described at II above, the rebuilding in replica of Georgian facades can very rarely be justified.

An exception might be made for the eccentric who requires a ' folly ' and wants to build a ' georgian ' house in the grand manner, on whim, as a replica of another which he admires; this course has, after all, ample precedent in the Renaissance.   Provided that the funds are available to do the job thoroughly, the results might be more or less acceptable.

However, there have been proposals for the building of whole terraces of ' georgian town houses ', with facades in replica, in areas within the canals, which is quite another matter.   This way lies potential disaster — all the more so if existing by-law setbacks and street-widths were adhered to.

The present rash of ' georgian ' housing estates and ' villages ' in the outer suburbs is faintly ridiculous, but relatively harmless to anyone but a demented purist.

A misguided policy-enforcement by Dublin Corporation planning department has resulted in a number of developments which have facades in near-replica with a modern office building behind, Dresden-style. This policy is deemed to keep the streetscape intact but it surely can please only the galloping horseman and the economist.   To the conscience-stricken, the almost total destruction of the integrity of the buildings far outweighs superficial conformity to the idiom of a streetscape; and the skylines, with obtrusively-visible and incongruous penthouses, are very disturbing.

This policy if it persisted could ultimately lead to absurdity and we would be left with a wild-west-saloon-front Dublin: the Dublin Urban Study of the year 2175 would make mournful reading for our descendants and our own shades.

This situation *has* arisen, fortunately on a small scale, in Leeson street and Harcourt street.   In the former, numbers 86, 87 and 88 have been rebuilt in this manner and numbers 83, 84, 85, although in perfectly sound condition, have a planning permission for a similar development, with the palliative of a pitifully small ' residential ' content in the office usage.

6.5   Vanished streetscape: Hume Street-St. Stephen's Green

6.6   Pastiche streetscape: Hume Street-St. Stephen's Green

Pastiche streetscape: Hume Street-St. Stephen's Green

6.7   Proposed termination of Fitzwilliam Place

Reproduction: Replica 2

Architects have to face problems where houses have been defaced by previous owners, far beyond the possibility of restorative undoing at *any* cost.

Where this applies to three or more units in a streetscape and whatever usage is permitted or proposed, replica or pastiche 'georgian' is not acceptable. There are agonizing decisions to be made and sometimes considerations outside the torture of architecture influence the production of the wrong solution.

The south facade of Ely place was an almost intact intimate streetscape with rich historical seasoning. In 1910 the owners, a religious order, almost gutted and subdivided the interiors of numbers 2, 3 and 4; rendered (greycoat) the upper floor brick facades and oil-painted the granite ground-floor facings. The design of these facades is particularly interesting to the historian as the round-headed ground and first floor windows are very unusual in south-side Dublin, being copies, the writer thinks, of houses in the environs of Fitzroy square, London.

The proposed rebuilding in (fairly exact) replica (see 6.3) with offices behind, for which planning permission has been obtained, is the wrong solution. However, number 1, on the corner with Baggot street, is now to be demolished by Dublin Corporation for road-widening, so a modern scheme, nobly to terminate Ely place and subtley to turn the corner, is a possibility.

When the building of Fitzwilliam street had eventually progressed uphill to Leeson street, the idiom had begun to tire of itself. The c. 1840 facades had coarsened and the details tended to the mechanical. Drawing 6.7 shows a proposal (abortive) for terminating the great streetscape with an anonymous mirror building. No demolition was proposed (other than an edwardian mews) and the integrity and domestic usage of the existing building would have been maintained. Mammon would also have been served, to justify to the developer the (then) record price at auction for the site.

Reproduction: Pastiche

The writer feels *very* strongly that the insertion of pastiche facades, for whatever reason of client or local authority requirement, is positively wrong and destructive of the very values which it lamely tries to save or with which it strives to keep-in-keeping: it is a simulacrum of everything that the 18th century builders achieved.

A Classical (?) Example of this is the destruction of a marvellous group of relatively sound, important, splendid irreplaceable buildings at the junction of Hume street and Saint Stephen's green, by means which are now unsavoury history and their replacement by pastiche of poor quality, with a disastrous skyline. A comparison of the "before and after" photographs, aided by memory, may show what has been lost.

Some case may of course be made for eclecticism within the broad grammar of a style, as those familiar with the works of Norman Shaw will know. But architecture based on the gratuitous assembly of dead parts, however expertly manipulated, will just not do in our beautiful city: the existing standards of the real thing are too high and have been too splendidly abetted by Time.

6.8 *Facade restored: 6 South Leinster Street*

6.9 *Facade restored: 65 Lower Baggot Street*

6.10 *Facade restored: 7 Lower Fitzwilliam Street*

6.11 *Facade restored: 18 Lower Baggot Street*

6.12 *A new manifestation—Victorian pastiche: Elgin Road*

56

Streets, Streetscapes and Traffic

by John Costello

7.2

7.1 *A safe and interesting junction, marred by untidy furniture*

Introduction

The intrusion of throughbound traffic is one of the most formidable problems threatening the visual and environmental value of our city. It is not necessary to expand here on the actual injury caused by traffic in terms of its noise, danger, dirt and visual intrusion. It is more important to examine the significance in the urban landscape of the street itself and the contribution that streetscape makes to our environment. It is this quality that is being eroded by traffic; and our society has constantly to choose between the needs of motorised transport and the values of urban environment.

The Street

The significance of 'the street' is twofold. In visual terms the street itself is part of the space that makes up the composition of an urban landscape; that connects in two dimensions, and in horizontal plane, the solid geometry of buildings; and that dictates the town's pattern—the disposition of buildings in relationship to each other. In terms of use, one of the functions of a street has always been as a means of *connection* between buildings as well as a method of transportation for through traffic.

The modern street, however, has been compared to a "river of vehicles", a dividing surface, not a connecting one. The balance between these two functions has often been lost and the efforts, for example, to pedestrianise streets and to divert traffic from our city's heart is one attempt to retrieve the street for the useful as well as for the visual benefit of our environment.

A major characteristic of the street is its capability for *change*. For better or for worse, we seem to be able to alter with relative ease the direction and character of existing streets as well as to create new routes. So, if we accept the environmental importance of these spaces we must underline the need for extreme care and study in decisions concerning traffic control and road proposals.

Separation of Traffic

Traffic is a very wide term; it can include pedestrians, cyclists, delivery vans, refuse trucks and other movements of people and vehicles which properly belong within the most enclosed city precinct. Heavy through traffic having no business in such areas, however, is altogether different; it is in W. K. MacKay's words ' merely another and more expensive form of sewage,' and must be treated in the same way—as a necessary evil which requires distasteful segregation.

Space at Traffic Intersections

Traffic intersections often result in the forming of "new" and sometimes useful land that has a part to play in the urban scene. In the past, this land was often used for visual effect—providing focal point sites, in the classical manner, for civic structures or major memorials of which Nelson Pillar was a notable example. But the land was also used for other less ambitious functional purposes—for instance, for lavatories, benches, tree planting, kiosks and horse troughs.

These are part of a town's useful 'furniture', and the sheer volume of present-day traffic cannot fully obscure the pleasantness of such places as those seen, for example, at Clanbrassil street and Monkstown.

Constant road 'improvements' continually create such space in today's city and suburbs. We take here just a few examples to examine its value:—

(a) The typical suburban 'roundabout' may have little amenity usefulness, but its broad and bleak scale can obviously be improved by planting.

(b) The centre city 'island' and surplus path-space can provide a usefulness, and the top end of Grafton street is an example of a modern, yet ancient, use of 'free' town space—as a place where people can meet, sit, view or exhibit their wares or works of art. Such spots tend to emerge ' naturally ' in an unplanned way; they may not easily be planned but they should be encouraged to develop naturally.

(c) The basic design aim in planning street intersections involves planning the safe movement of vehicles and of pedestrians; a street intersection is a complex of footpaths as well as of roads.

The new road arrangement beside the car ferry terminal building at Dunlaoghaire illustrates what proper urban design can achieve—a combination of functional success and visual distinction. In fact

57

7.3 The cars invade the footpath

the lesson is yet again the importance of minor detail and the part it can play.

Principles
Accordingly, design principles inherent in and common to the detailing of all streets and streetscape emerge as follows:

—Safe passage for Vehicles *and* for People
—Visual clarity and effect
—Potential use for civic or amenity purposes
—Respect for (existing) street pattern

Street Pattern
The Dublin Urban Study elsewhere emphasises the major significance of street pattern in defining our city's structure and character, recognising the impact of this space in the total composition. Public awareness and economics has lessened the threat of major disruptive road 'schemes' and motorways to the city's physical core and human character. Our problem for the moment, however, has been confined more to the subtle and less obvious damage caused by 'improvements' to existing streets and paths and to the lack of comprehensive design approach to the new suburban network that is being created, which in turn helps to affect the environment of our expanding city. The damage of 'improvements' is often the physical destruction of buildings as a result of road widening and their replacement by undifferentiated flat space. The end result is often the altering of scale, the creation of useless 'no-man's-land' and the effect of blight.

Damage to streets can be caused by other reasons: the Wolfe Tone statue disrupts the form of St. Stephen's green and is an intrusion. On the other hand, a lovely piece of urban sculpture (Oisin Kelly's group of figures designed for Liberty Hall) was refused permission on the grounds that it would (if you please!) 'disrupt' the pavement. Fortunately the citizens of Cork were more appreciative, and this splendid group now worthily adorns, not the second-tallest, but the tallest building in Ireland—Cork County Hall.

7.4 The trees help, but it is still a bit bleak

7.5 The unpopular pedestrian subway

The most notable disaster resulting from the destruction of Nelson Pillar is the street space and attendant 'furniture' that now exists opposite the G.P.O.

New Buildings
The arrangement of street change has a major influence on the disposition of *new* building. The establishment of new building lines often occur as a result of decisions about traffic and not about urban landscaping. An entire streetscape can alter radically and disastrously.

New buildings also can in turn themselves influence streetscape—the courtyard (or 'well') of large developments, which arise from the building's size, are often merely twilight 'public' spaces; sometimes such space could become a part of, and an extension to, the street or path pattern. To take an outward turning example, the American embassy has created a worthwhile streetscape environment.

The ground floor treatment of city building is relevant; a major problem today is the sheer dullness caused

7.6 Good detailing and careful retention of trees

7.7 The pedestrian is king again

7.10 Genuine Victorian charm

7.8 A quiet cul-de-sac

7.9 Meters are clumsy and expensive

by the solid or screened ground floor front. Obviously, this is connected with use-decisions; but a sympathetic design treatment can help relieve the lack of visual interest.

Street Surface

A street is not therefore a neutral part of the urban landscape. In terms of its own physical appearance the street, due to its size or location, can in itself possess an aesthetic value—in its shape, line, texture and detail; an alleyway or a motorway equally can possess these qualities. The street is a surface and can be described as a sort of *carpet*. Concrete and asphalt are the materials used in our age—perhaps a future technology will discover that these materials can develop the colour and texture that we associate, say, with paving and cobbles? In any event, concrete properly handled, *can* look well, and the use of paths, kerbs, levels, varied textures and, above all, the use of grass and growing ground cover offers considerable opportunity to the designer.

' Furniture '

The sheer confusion of traffic often conceals the detailed elements that also stand on the ' carpet '— aptly described as ' street furniture ': lamps, signs, meters, seats, monuments, shelters, litter-bins, kiosks, advertisements, traffic signs. It is obviously beyond human endeavour to plan and co-ordinate all these elements—they tend to occur suddenly and to disappear as quickly. It is, however, of importance to recognise both their value and their potential visual destructiveness, particularly in cases where control can be achieved. The traffic meter is a case in point— ugly in itself, the cause of parked vehicles and the reason why (say) Merrion square's vista can now be enjoyed only at weekends. Again the example of Cork might have been followed with profit; the parking discs now used in that city are not only more flexible and economical in use than meters, they also give to the streets a clean-shaven appearance which is so sadly lacking in present-day Dublin on Sunday mornings.

Landscape

There are two further important elements that have always been used in decorating our streetscape, notably for landscaping and boundaries. The use of

trees is a human response to city environment; it is also a method that provides a scale and a contrasting screen to buildings. Dublin is full of empty space that cries aloud either for high deciduous trees or low-scale clustered planting, or both.

' Boundaries '

Street boundaries include the kerbs, railings, fencings, bollards or walls that enclose the foreground of a street. These contribute to the line of a street or a path and, moreover, they constitute the intimate details that a pedestrian can perceive. The butchery of railings and their replacement, if at all, by foot-high blockwork is a further intrusion. Boundary walls and gates enclose our new suburban paths—normally in a primitive design manner, but sometimes (as in the housing estate at Clonkeen) with interest and variation.

Usefulness

The enjoyment and the usefulness of streets for purposes other than traffic has almost been forgotten. Despite our climate, this space *can* be used for relaxation, for trading and for other urban activity. The plea for pedestrianisation, combined with off-street parking, is not a romantic search for the past. But we cannot study pedestrianisation as a single issue—the enjoyment of the urban scene is fundamentally linked up with our decision about economics, city growth, commerce and, above all, a co-ordinated transport policy.

In the meanwhile, some steps can be considered:
    Re-open Grafton street to the pedestrian?
    Remove the cars entirely from Fitzwilliam square?
    Replace Moore street?
    Construct shopping kiosks and gradually designate the area between George's street and Grafton street as roofed, pedestrianised shopping areas?

Policy

But the most necessary step is for our city to recognise the significance and potential of both new and old streets; and the fact that street design is not confined to the problems of traffic. The traffic engineer and the administration that between them make the decisions on traffic have a responsibility in the changing and improvement of our city.

7.11 *Suburban peace and quiet*

7.14 *Building and street combine together in harmony to the benefit of the pedestrian*

7.12 *Quiet—until the commuters come*

7.15 *All day, every day—the cars*

The greatest need here is to co-ordinate traffic study in all its aspects with the overall planning and environmental problems of Dublin, and to consider individual problems as a design challenge related equally to people and environment as well as to the motor vehicle.

7.16 *A Pembroke lampstandard*

7.13 *Here to stay: the Supermarket*

City Housing Improvement

by Shane de Blacam and Loughlin Kealy

The Case Study

The study deals with nineteenth-century houses within the boundary formed by the Grand and Royal canals. Seven districts of these houses are identified. The Heytesbury street district was selected as the location for the case study. Conclusions and proposals are put forward.

Contents

There follows an edited summary of the study.

1. Introduction

The residential areas of the city are under pressure from the changing demands on space in the city and the aging of their building fabric.

Perhaps the change most difficult to assess is one which is a product of the city's growth and its need for a new kind of workforce. The response of the city to this need results in functional changes in different areas, which in turn may lead to environmental and building decay. The case-study area still has a residential function, but this function is altering. The area is in demand as a prime location for flats and bedsitters. Its population seems to be shifting from a family-dominated one to one where young transients form a considerable proportion. The needs of the latter may well be met here—but these needs are not the same as those of families. There is evidence that the area is deficient in some facilities required by a family-structured population. Here then is one sector where a policy decision on the future role of the area is required. Such a decision will involve an examination of the houses in terms of suitability for different population-groups and an assessment of the desirable mix. In this regard it must be noted that, while environmental and building decay can be combated, deterioration of a community poses a far more difficult problem. It should also be noted that in areas such as that studied, the persistence of the community has in all probability meant that environmental decay has not kept pace with building deterioration. A decision, then, on the role of the area in relation to the city will determine the form and extent of any possible intervention.

2. The Method of the Case Study

The work fell into two stages—the first concerned with assessment of the area in terms of its social and physical character and the changes taking place within it, the second with an examination of improvement options for typical house forms, and with suggested upgrading of part of area now under particular stress in that it has been designated "obsolete" by Dublin Corporation.

The first stage involved preliminary examination and analysis, and set out to provide the groundwork for more detailed study. Information on population figures and trends, age-structures and employment, housing-types and dates, condition and occupancy was taken from the Census of Population, 1971.

The study area comprises all of one electoral ward, Wood Quay B, and portion of another, St. Kevin's. The data from Wood Quay B ward was used as being indicative of conditions typical of the study area. St. Kevin's ward extends to Leeson street, so that a comparatively small proportion of its area falls within the study area.

A survey of land use and building condition and a photographic survey were undertaken. Reference data were also abstracted from the 1973 edition of Thom's Dublin Street Directory. Interviews were held with representatives of community organisations active in the area, the Eastern Health Board social worker responsible for the area, and the local clergy.

The second stage involved an analysis of a section of the study area. This analysis provides an estimate of the condition and facilities of the type of housing under review. A full survey was made of three houses typical of the case study area in order to examine their capacity for modification and improvement. Proposals for these house-improvements were made, and costs were analysed. Assessments of street patterns and traffic movements were also made.

3. Physical Characteristics of the Case Study Area

The case study area comprises 168 acres. It extends from Clanbrassil street to Camden street and from Long lane and Camden row to the Grand canal. It is almost flat, with a slight fall towards its northern boundary.

The area is predominantly residential, other uses occurring for the most part on the boundary streets. It contains some 1,120 houses. Of these 13% are now multi-unit dwellings. Although most buildings are over one hundred years old, the area in general has been well maintained.

The majority of the buildings in the study area were built between 1850 and 1890. They were built on farm land between the Grand canal and the Liberties of the city; they do not conform to a grand design for the area, but were built in short terraces and sections of terraces by many separate private builders, by institutions, and by a public company.

The private builders erected several houses at a time, conforming to a building line and making *streets* with narrow service lanes at the rear. There are single and two storey cottages, and one and two storey over basement houses, often with front planting three to ten feet deep. The houses of the Dublin Artisan Dwelling Company are almost back-to-back in narrow streets, with no front planting.

Variation of design and builder but similarity of scale makes for a surprising variety of streets of different lengths, culs-de-sac and small terraces with common front spaces or gardens.

The area is bisected by the fifty-foot-wide south circular road, along which were built more grand two, three and four storey houses, shops and churches.

An area of particular interest is around Harty place and Daniel street. It was noted in the course of the study that these houses had been declared obsolete by Dublin Corporation. Over the years the Dublin Artisan Dwelling Company have maintained these buildings to a higher standard than many of the

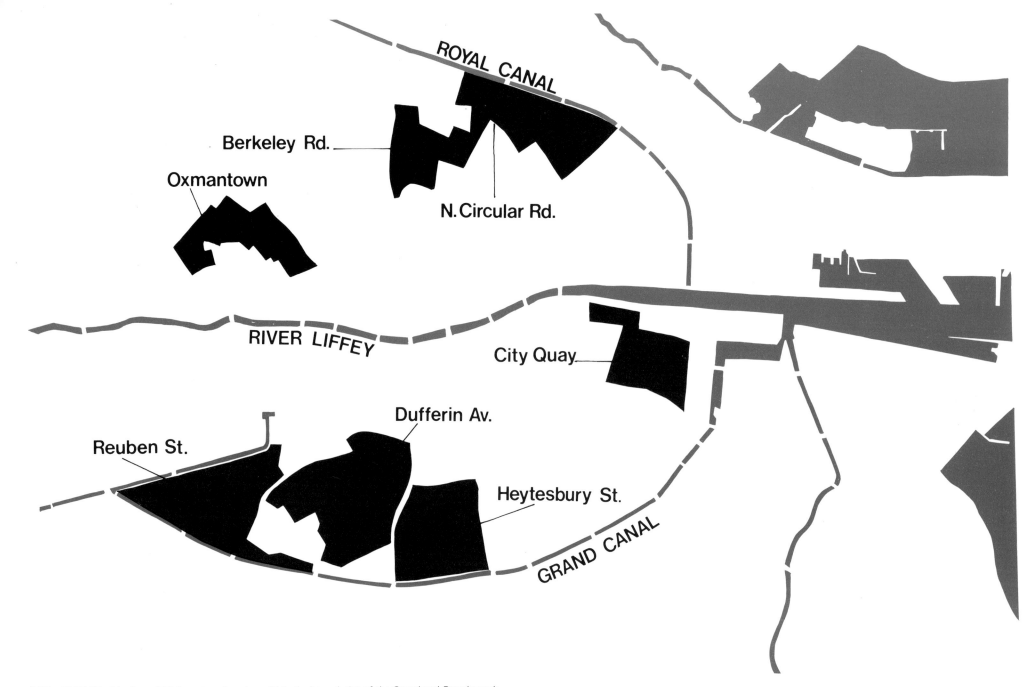

8.01   DUBLIN: Districts of 19th century housing within the boundaries of the Grand and Royal canals

buildings in the study area. It is a conclusion of the study that these 120 houses should be improved and the environment upgraded.

Heavy traffic within the area is for the most part confined to the south circular road and, to a lesser extent, Heytesbury street. The boundary streets— Camden, Clanbrassil and Kevin—are major traffic routes.

The Dublin Development Plan of 1971 indicates that the area will remain predominantly residential. A number of terraces in Heytesbury street and Synge street and two historic buildings—Portobello House and the Gascoigne Home—have been listed for preservation.

Road proposals for the area indicate that Camden street and Clanbrassil street will both become even more important traffic arteries in the immediate future. The Clanbrassil street roadway developments will cause the demolition of seven small commercial properties in the study area. The Grand canal scheme of January 1975 shows that carriageway along Porto-

bello road will affect buildings along Windsor terrace and Portobello harbour. This scheme provides for some amenity open space.

There are two primary schools in the study area, CBS Synge street school for boys, and Zion school in Bloomfield avenue. Part of the Kevin street College of Technology is also in the area. Three religious denominations have places of worship here. Harrington street church serves the Catholic population while the Church of Ireland has a church in Bloomfield avenue. There is a synagogue in Walworth road serving the Jewish community.

There are over one hundred and twenty retail shops in the study area. Of these a quarter are general food stores. They are concentrated mainly along the traffic routes of Camden street/Richmond street south and Clanbrassil street. The rest are scattered among the residential blocks. There are no large retail units or supermarkets.

In the Study Area as a whole there are about 55 industrial premises. These concerns vary widely in

nature, the most common being engineering works, furniture and drapery manufacturing. Firms are for the most part small-scale operations and are concentrated in the south (Grand canal) and east (Camden street) sectors, often being located in back lanes.

There is no public open space in the study area, apart from the banks of the canal which are used as play-areas by the children. There are some parks close by—the ' lawn ' off Charlemont street, and St. Kevin's park adjacent to the College of Technology. A floodlit hard football ground has been proposed for Griffith square, which is also close to the area.

Over half of the housing units are owner-occupied, while a quarter are rented unfurnished from private landlords. The remainder are either rented from the local authority or else held free of rent.

While most of the dwellings are in fair condition, it is apparent that multiple-occupancy dwellings, and those located near major traffic routes, tend to be less well maintained.

8.02　CASE STUDY AREA: The area of this study extends from Clanbrassil Street to Camden Street and from Long Lane to Grand Canal

8.04　Bloomfield Avenue: Corner shop on the Grand Canal

8.05　Bloomfield Avenue: Two storey red brick houses

8.03　Windsor Terrace: Single storey houses facing south to the Grand Canal

8.06　Windsor Terrace: Two storey houses

63

8.07 Bloomfield Park: Off Ringstand Parade

8.09 Walworth Road: Short two storey e/w terrace of red brick

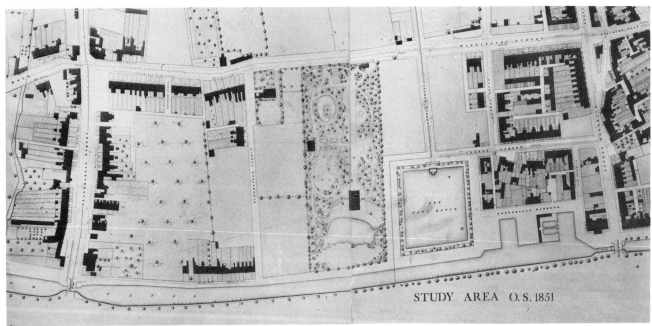

STUDY AREA O.S. 1851

8.10 Case-Study Area: from Ordnance Survey Map dated 1851

8.11 Lennox Street

Major deficiencies

In the sample taken for detailed study, it was noted that dampness was a major problem, originating both from the original construction of the houses without a damp proof course, and from the subsequent failure of elements of the building, such as roof coverings, gutters and valleys.

The most obvious deficiency in amenity is that of public space. While the canal bank can be so described, it does not provide a suitable recreational area for children. In any event, it is isolated from the greater part of the residential area by a major traffic route, the south circular road. This deficiency is rendered more acute by the fact that very many of the smaller dwellings have little private open spaces available to them. If these dwellings were to be extended, such ground as was available is likely to be further reduced. The dwellings require extension to provide essential facilities without further restricting their limited internal space. The area as a whole needs to yield additional open space. It is likely that its needs can be met by small pockets of open space, designed for recreation and amenity.

The proposal for Griffith square to which reference is made above goes hardly any distance towards meeting the need for public open space, and can have only marginal value in relation to the area as a whole.

The Dublin Artisan Dwelling Company has recently adopted a policy of selling their houses either to existing tenants, or on the open market as they become available.

4. Social Characteristics of the Case Study Area

Population figures for the Wood Quay B Ward indicate a decline in population of 4.3% between 1966 and 1971. Comparisons with other Inner City residential areas show this to be fairly low. For example, North of the river Liffey —

Mountjoy A Ward fell by 19%, and
Mountjoy B Ward fell by almost 16%.

During the same period, the average for Dublin City showed a 31% increase, against a national average increase of 3.3%.

Age structures show some considerable deviations from national averages. The age group 0-14 comprises 19.8% of the Ward's population, as compared to a national figure of 29.5%. The age group 20-24 comprises 14.4% of the total compared to 7.3% nationally. These figures suggest a decrease in family occupancy and an increase in the number of young flatdwellers.

The unemployment figure of 2.1% is low compared to the national average of 5.8%. The statistics also indicate that the female workforce is very high.

Of the working population of Wood Quay B Ward, 60% are employed in industry. The figure for St. Kevin's Ward is 57%.

Community Organisations

Several community organisations are active in the area. The principal focus of activity is the organisation of

64

8.12   No. 3 Avoca Road and No. 14 Emor Street

recreational facilities, directed in the main at young people, although there are also a number of groups catering for adults and for the needs of the elderly.

The main problems that these groups encounter is lack of space in which to hold meetings and functions. Youth clubs are at present working in garages which are on temporary loan to them, but space is cramped and inadequate. Children involved in sports have to travel quite a distance in order to play or practise.

The Garda club in Harrington street is used for bingo and occasional social functions; but there are no other community or parish halls and no dance halls, although the latter is hardly a problem in an area so close to the city centre. The various community organisations and youth clubs provide some facilities for those aged between five and twenty years including sports training, table tennis, and classes in chess, crafts and music.

The girl guides' association in Harrington street has a hall which is occasionally loaned to other groups in the area to use for specific functions.

5.   Detailed Analysis of the Houses

In order to establish precise information on the condition of the houses, a portion of the case study area was chosen for detailed investigation. This was the Dublin Artisan Dwelling Company single-storey houses around Harty place and the split-level houses on Vernon street, McMahon street and the north side of Lombard street west. It covers 233 houses on 7.4 acres (almost 31.5 dwellings per acre) and a sample survey of one in six houses was carried out. This condition-survey covered the building fabric as well as facilities. The information was gathered by means of a questionnaire plus a visual survey, completed by the inspecting architect in conjunction with the occupant of the house.

Two house-types predominate; these are the Dublin Artisan Dwelling Company one-storey houses of Harty place and Daniel street, and the large split-level houses in Lombard street west and McMahon street. The artisan houses are generally better maintained than the split-level privately-owned houses, although a few of the latter have been completely renovated. All houses have small back yards, many with lean-to and

8.14   No. 34 St. Kevins Parade

8.15   No. 33 Synge St. Birthplace of George Bernard Shaw

8.16   No. 8 and No. 9 Carlisle Street

65

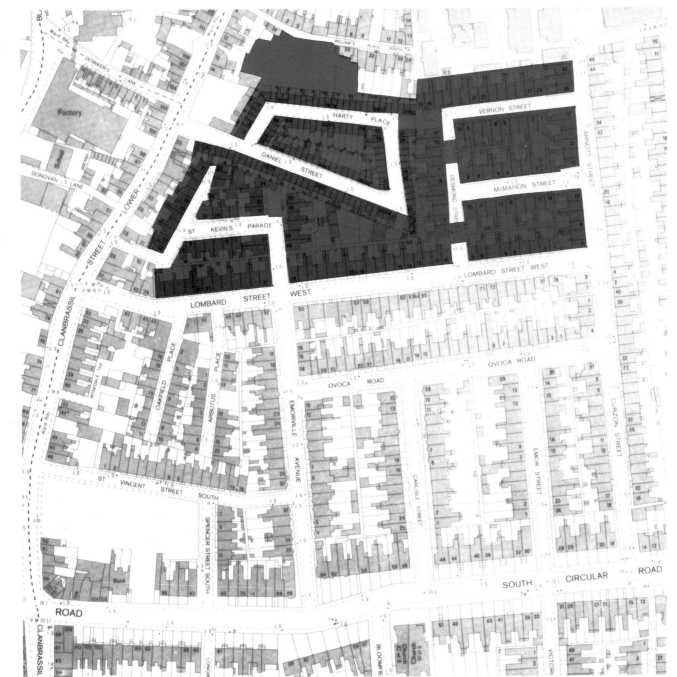

8.29 Portion of case-study area: Single-storey houses, Harty Place—Daniel St.; split level, Lombard St. W., Vernon St., McMahon St.

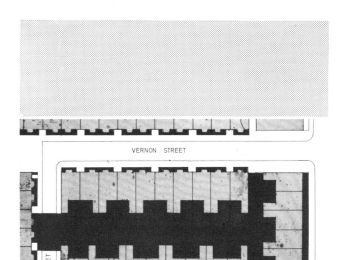

8.32 Plan of McMahon St./Vernon St. Block: Split-level houses

8.33 Rear access lane of Lombard Street West

8.30 McMahon Street

8.31 Lombard St. West

other sheds in bad condition. The artisan cottages do not have rear access; the access lanes to the split-level houses are in very bad condition.

One Storey House

66% of these have rising damp problems. Only 15% of these houses have minimum bathroom facilities. The gutters are in reasonable state of repair, but 70% of the slates are in fair to poor condition.

Split-level houses

These houses were built without a damp proof course at ground level; as a result 73% had serious dampness problems. 54% of the houses have roof slates in poor condition, and in 77% the gutters are faulty. In some cases the rear gutters have been replaced but the front gutters cannot be renewed except at considerable expense because the type required is no longer available. The valley gutter running the length of the terrace needs renewal. Other problems encountered were the poor condition of brick pointing, the fact that several houses are without a flue liner, and the use of brick nogging partition walls.

8.17 Split-Level house about Lombard Street West

8.21 Two storey house (D.A.D. Co.)

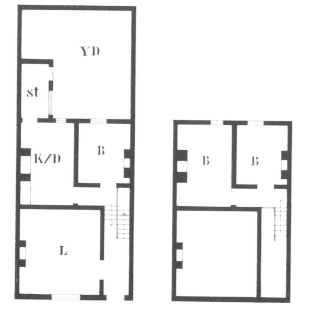

Existing house

1. Split-Level House

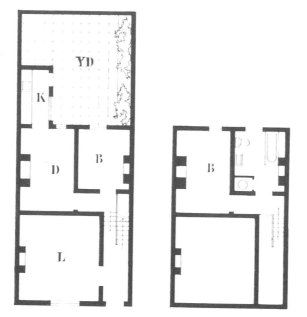

Basic level improvement

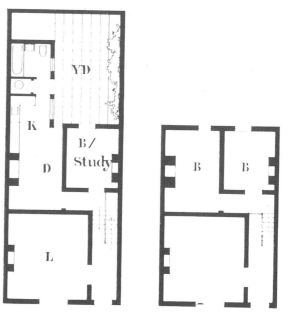

2nd. level improvement

Summary of findings

1. 70% of the houses have dampness at ground floor level
2. 50% are without minimum sanitary facilities
3. 75% of the houses, other than the artisan cottages, have serious slate and gutter problems.

The residents of the houses were asked what improvements they would like made to their houses if there were substantial grants available. 70% of those without bathrooms said they would be interested in building one. Other suggestions included new roof tiles, larger kitchens and some means of keeping the dampness away. In the split-level houses, 70% expressed the need for new gutters and a renewal of the brick pointing.

In the artisan cottages, only one resident was interested in an additional bedroom.

33% of the residents from all of houses surveyed did not feel the need for any improvements; a majority of these were old people who felt it would be too troublesome and hardly worth it at their age.

6. Improvement Plans for the Houses

Apart from those pressures outlined earlier which stem from the functional change of the area in relation to the city, deficiencies of fabric and amenity threaten the survival of the whole community.

Fabric deficiencies in the houses surveyed are of two kinds: those that concern the soundness of the buildings and those that stem from a change in required standards of accommodation. It has been noted that most of the buildings in the area appear basically sound.

A complete survey of three specimen houses was made. These were:

1. The split level house.
2. The single storey house of the Dublin Artisan Dwelling Company.
3. The two storey house of the Dublin Artisan Dwelling Company.

Proposals for two kinds of improvement are made.

Proposed Improvements

First, minimum improvements which involves provision of essentials—hot water supply, w.c., bath, wash-hand basin, damp-proofing at ground floor, re-wiring, general repairs and re-decoration.

Second—alternative improvements which include the above but involve new work outside the existing walls of the house. The estimate of cost of each improvement-plan was made by a quantity surveyor and was based on traditional methods of construction by a small general contractor. These costs are based on February 1975 prices and they have not altered at the time of publication.

Split Level House:

Minimum improvement	£2,950
Alternative improvement	£3,350

Single Storey House:

Minimum improvement	
South front	£1,300
South back	£1,450
Alternative improvement	£2,800

Two Storey House:

Minimum improvement £2,000
Alternative improvement £2,575

These figures represent a fraction of the financial cost of the provision of new housing. If improvements are not made, the building fabric will continue to deteriorate and eventually reach a point beyond which it cannot be repaired. Large scale re-development will be necessary and with it the high social cost of sudden disruption of a community. Current housing policy, with its exclusive concentration on achieving the maximum number of new houses annually, does not favour the improvement of the existing housing stock. That policy urgently needs total re-appraisal.

7. The Environment

The basic physical urban form in the case study area is the *street* of terraced houses. A particular example of this is illustrated in the Vernon street/McMahon street block, with split-level houses having small front garden to the street, back to private yard, and rear access lane. There is a potential traffic hazard in the

they provide by way of dwelling and the street environment.

This outline study has concerned itself with one such area. A number of factors arise from this examination which are relevant to improvement intervention both in the area studied and in similar areas elsewhere.

The first consideration is that the improvements required are beyond the financial capacity of the great majority of the present occupants of the area. Many of the owner/occupiers consider that the basic improvements described earlier are not justifiable in view of the expected short term of their occupancy. Nevertheless the fabric requires maintenance and improvement if widespread dereliction is to be avoided and the area in question is to be suitable for residence.

The second consideration concerns the strategy of improvement. At first sight it might seem that the simplest option would be for the local authority to acquire property for rehabilitation. Experience in Britain, however, suggests that blanket compulsory purchase, while still feasible in total clearance opera-

8.25 One-Storey house (D.A.D. Company)

9. Proposals

Two general proposals are put forward as a basis for intervention.

Improvement Areas

Government action is required to make provision for Improvement Areas in the City.

There are a number of constituent factors involved in programmes relating to such areas which require a legal framework for their effective operation. Included in these are:

Increased direct grants to individuals for improvements;

Provision for group finance schemes;

Provision of temporary housing.

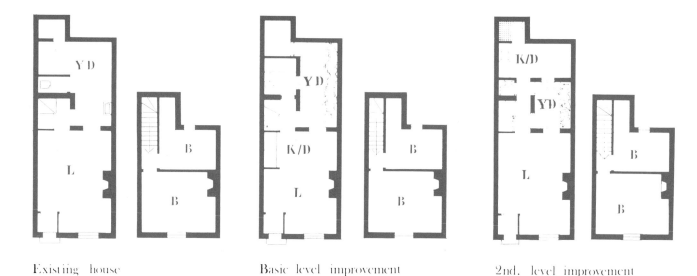

Existing house   Basic level improvement   2nd. level improvement

3. Two Storey House: Built by the Dublin Artisan Dwelling Company near Lennox Street

street but, away from the main Camden street, Clanbrassil street and south circular road traffic-ways, the vehicular movement is generated only by local need. The street/house/yard/lane relationship seems to work well. New pavement and street-lighting on the rear access lane could provide traffic-free play areas. Restrictions on through traffic by bollards and tree planting on one half of one-way streets and maintenance of the small existing green spaces are further environmental improvements that need to be made.

8. Conclusions

It is imperative that the inner residential areas of Dublin be maintained and developed. Much of the areas involved were originally constructed at about the same time. Consequently they are aging simultaneously. Although considerable variations in condition occur, due in part to the different circumstances of ownership or tenancy, in general these areas are now in need of attention both with respect to the kind of residential function they serve, and to the amenity

tions, defeats many of the purposes of an improvement policy, and throws the entire burden of planning, administration and finance on to the local authority. Compulsory purchase itself is of necessity a tedious and protracted process. Consequently it tends to be applied to substantial parcels of land, bringing about large-scale displacement which would rupture the community, thereby adding heavy social costs to the required financial outlay.

Programmes designed for areas where such improvement is undertaken must encompass the requirements of fabric and facilities improvement, the provision of amenity areas, and special financial provisions. They require a management factor in order to avoid unnecessary disruption while work is in progress, including the provision of alternative accommodation for those temporarily displaced.

It is evident that such programmes require the active co-operation of the community for their implementation.

Organisation: Improvement Agency

A special task force is required in each Improvement Area to establish liaison with the community, and to determine with the community the nature and extent of improvements. A legal framework is required through which this task force could act on behalf of the community organisation. These task forces would form part of an Area Improvement Agency whose function it would be to administer the operations. This agency might be either a section of Dublin Corporation's Community and Environment Department, or an independent organisation funded from Local or Central Government.

City Housing Redevelopment

by James Pike

Introduction

In central Dublin within the canals there were once many clearly-defined local communities, each with a special life of its own. Various pressures, both historical and economic, have wiped out many of these communities; but some still survive. The enforced or threatened breakdown of these surviving communities cries out for remedy.

The arguments in favour of central-city living are well known, and do not need to be re-stated; but the means of ensuring continuity for those communities which still survive, and for the re-introduction of people into areas already blighted or threatened with blight, need closer study.

The dwindling and threatened communities can be classified in many ways, but for the purposes of this study they can be considered under two broad headings:

1. Areas made up predominantly of buildings less than 100 years old, the majority of which, either because of better standards of construction initially, or better maintenance, or both, provide a physically valuable contribution to the housing stock. Here the policy should basically be that of re-instatement, modernisation and consolidation.

2. Other areas, mostly though not entirely consisting of buildings over 100 years old, where age and poor maintenance have combined to render the majority of buildings at best obsolescent, at worst gone far beyond the point where they can usefully be retrieved or retained at all.

The first of these two categories has been dealt with in the Heytesbury Street study by Shane de Blacam and Loughlin Kealy. The present paper is primarily concerned with the second type of area—that is, one of comprehensive residential re-development on a central-city site.

Economics of City-centre Housing

By crude economic standards only, housing in central-city areas cannot be justified in comparison with returns obtainable from non-residential uses. Such standards should not, however, be the sole criterion; the total health, social as well as economic, of the fabric of the city must be the concern of the planning authority. The closer the housing lies to the heart of the city, the greater the economic problem becomes; and this fact, although well known, must carefully be considered by the local authorities in their land use zoning for central city areas.

Historically, central-city owners have regarded it as a matter of right that the highest development potential should be bestowed on their lands, leaving the less profitable uses—i.e. residential, social and open-space —to be banished outward to the surrounding suburbs. There is here a direct clash of ideologies which can only be resolved, as far as these central city areas are concerned, by one of the following three courses of action:

(a) Acceptance of the historical and more recent *status quo* which would mean no positive action on centre city housing;

(b) Multi-purpose zoning of land, regardless of possible hardship to individual owners; or

(c) Acceptance of the *status quo*, but committing the local authority to a policy of central city re-development, plus a commitment to pay non-residential prices for central-city land which they need for residential use.

In the short-term at least, alternative (c) appears to be the only practicable one. Attempts to introduce a residential component into mixed development, while it may achieve an arithmetical addition to the housing stock, is not the way in which to create or revive real urban communities. It, no doubt, makes a worthwhile contribution to total housing stock; but of its very nature, housing which is combined with office or commercial development tends to attract the more highly mobile and transient elements of the population, especially bachelors of both sexes; and without the back-up of family housing close at hand, within the same parish or community, it can make little contribution to the problem here being discussed.

Clearly, in the long-term, alternative (b) must be regarded as the only real solution in overriding social terms. Equitable means of resolving this problem will have to be found; but such aspects of the problem are outside the scope of this paper. One thing is clear, however, at present, and for at least the immediate future: central city housing is unlikely to be profitable to, or provided by, the private sector in any significant quantity. The burden of its provision will continue to fall mainly on the shoulders of the local authority.

Density Assessment

Measurement of residential density, described by William Holford as "an arithmetical substitute for creative thinking", is not of itself an index of quality. Where dilapidation has occurred, with multiple lettings of small units in existing properties, once designed for more spacious living (the notorious tenements of the past) high densities can indeed be synonymous with low standards; but this is not necessarily so across the board of an entire residential community.

Past thinking on densities has been further bedevilled with majority needs, those especially of the "average" family, without proper reference to the very wide range of need within any community, from the single person (old or young), on the one hand, right up to the large family on the other.

It can safely be said that a housing programme which caters only for the average family is doomed to failure, since it provides uneconomically for the smaller household and in a damaging social way (because of over-

9.1   *Intimate urban scale should be retained*

9.2   *Housing stock worth conserving*

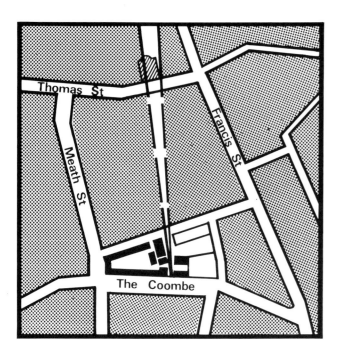

9.9   New pedestrian way preserves vista

crowding) for the larger household. Answering a wide variety of needs implies a great variety in both sizes and types of dwelling; the provision of a varying number of dwellings within the range of single bedroom to five or even six bedrooms, plus appropriate daytime and sanitary accommodation.

The fallacy of equating high density with poor conditions has been mentioned above; there is a counter-fallacy which is, that dramatic increases in density in new developments make a very significant contribution towards saving land, and that therefore, especially in the context of expensive centre city land, the highest

possible densities consistent with residential comfort should be aimed at.

This argument is fallacious on two grounds, one social and the other arithmetical. The social dangers of predominantly high-rise housing need only be mentioned in passing, since there is a growing awareness throughout the world that many prestigious high-rise projects have been socially disastrous for their occupants and for the community of which they form part. The arithmetical fallacy needs further elaboration.

If the dwelling component alone is considered, then the relationship between increased density and saving of land is a straight-line one; dwellings at 100 people per acre use one-fifth of the land necessary for dwellings at 20 people per acre, and so on. This ignores the fundamental distinction, however, between net and gross residential density. To quote from H.M.S.O. paper on Residential Densities, "the amount of land needed for open space, schools, etc., depends on the number of people living in the area and not the amount of land taken up by their homes. Therefore as densities increase these other requirements bulk larger and larger in total land needed, and the benefit from increased housing density becomes less and less".

Diminishing Returns

This ' law of diminishing returns ' is illustrated by the diagram opposite. On the basis of 1,000 people to be housed, the graph is plotted to provide a constant 4 acres per 1,000 for open space, and 4 further acres for primary schools, local roads, shops and other community facilities. It may be argued that both these standards are somewhat low and were they increased to, say, 10 acres overall (for all residential land uses other than that for actual dwellings), the diminishing returns demonstrated by the graph would be even more dramatic.

The Liberties Study

There follows an assessment, complementary to the Heytesbury Street study, of some of the factors which have arisen in connection with the re-development proposal for the Liberties area of Dublin—a project commissioned from the National Building Agency by Dublin Corporation to develop the lands contained within the Coombe/Newmarket C.P.O. area.

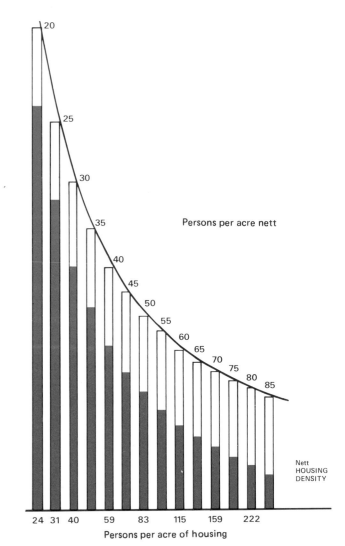

9.5   Increasing densities—diminishing land savings

Existing Features of the Area
Squares

These are admirable, satisfactorily providing many of the compensations of city life; but they have inherited shortcomings, due to the nature of the facilities provided. In the context of the problems of the day in which they were built, they provided excellent facilities; but by modern standards they require improvement.

The theme of making good the shortfalls which clearly present themselves must be studied critically, examined and developed, choosing as a typical example Brabazon Square, one of the many 19th century squares off the Coombe.

The spaces provided in these squares are human in scale and provide ideal environments for the creation of sub-communities, which relate to each other so as to contribute obviously to the strength of an overall community in the Liberties which (arguably) is the area of our city most vibrant with life.

Analysis of this and other squares shows an average of 40 dwellings per acre, made up of 2-storey and 1-storey houses. With an average occupancy of four persons per dwelling, the density is 160 persons per acre. In other examples, these densities are exceeded.

The shortfalls in the development are in the lack of kitchens and bathrooms. The provision in the yard space of these necessary rooms effectively eliminates the private outdoor space. One- and two-storey developments, if they are to cater fully for people's needs, must be developed at a lower density.

If, on the other hand, we retain the best of the existing elements and make up the shortcomings, we can construct two- and three-storey houses and four-storey maisonettes at high density, while retaining adequate open space and provision for car parking. Sunlight factors, noise reduction and existing site conditions are evaluated and linked with design decisions to determine the optimum form of development.

Many recent housing schemes for local authorities are constructed in the suburbs, as two-storey houses at up to 18 dwellings per acre, giving a density of 90 persons per acre. These developments are self-evidently inappropriate for urban development; for example, a 6-block of two-storey houses with 20 foot front gardens on the Coombe would be inappropriate. The residential building-form of the Coombe area of Dublin is three-storey (occasionally four-storey) directly fronting on to the main streets.

Construction of appropriate three-storey housing and four-storey maisonettes can obviously increase the density above the figure of 100 persons per acre. To achieve a higher density than 130 persons per acre requires the construction of medium rise developments which are not compatible with the general housing areas of Dublin city centre. Apart from the adverse economic factors described above the most serious criticism of medium-rise developments undertaken here or abroad is the lack of clear relationship between the individual dwellings and the ground. This can be achieved by three-storey houses while preserving the city road patterns and creating spaces for living, off the main streets.

By applying these measures to developments on any urban site, a density of between 110 and 130 per acre can be achieved while preserving human scale and achieving good environmental quality.

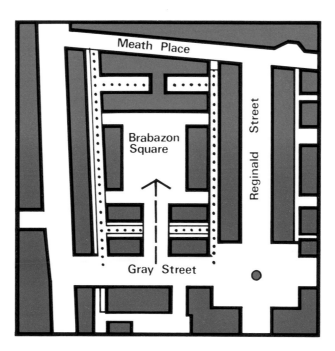

9.6   Intimate 19th century square

Brabazon Square

9.7   New development echoes traditional forms

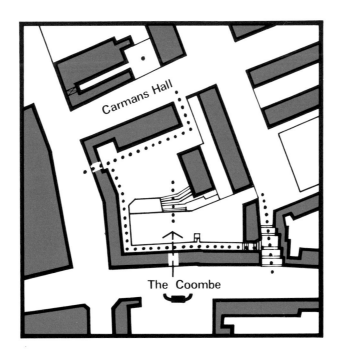

Car Parking

The amount of car parking in centre city residential areas can be determined by reference to assessments of present and future requirements.

There are two main sources of data on vehicle ownership in the Dublin area, viz. returns of the National Census and the Dublin Transportation Study (D.T.S.).

The Existing Position
a) Census Data

The Liberties are situated in Merchants Quay wards.

The following Table is extracted from the 1971 Census returns, in respect of Merchants Quay wards B and C.

Ownership Level	Income Level						
	1	2	3	4	5	6	7
0	96	73	58	48	41	36	32
1	4	27	41	47	47	44	43
2+	—	—	1	5	12	20	25

b) D.T.S. Data

The following Table extracted from the D.T.S. shows the percentage of households owning 0, 1 and 2+ vehicles at different income levels in High Density areas in 1970.

Ownership Level	Income Level						
	1	2	3	4	5	6	7
0	80	63	52	42	36	29	20
1	20	37	45	46	45	39	30
2+	—	—	3	12	19	32	50

By comparing the above Tables, it will be noted that the present car ownership in the Merchants Quay area corresponds to an income level between 1 and 2 at zero ownership level. While this reflects a 'statistical' rather than a 'real' position, it confirms the low car-ownership in the area suggested by other independent observations.

Projected Data

The D.T.S. Table with the corresponding data for 1991 is as follows (% households):

Ward	Total Pop.	Persons in house-holds	House-holds	Cars	% households without cars
B	2,955	2,857	908	170	81.3
C	2,893	2,581	747	108	85.6

As it self-evidently is not a function of residential areas to provide parking facilities for commercial or industrial uses, the maximum car parking required, and therefore to be provided, is 50%, plus some addition for visitors' cars. Indoor accommodation is primarily for people; the car should be encouraged to remain out-of-doors.

Traffic

The developing pattern of traffic and its conflict with living accommodation suggests very many possibilities which, if explored and developed to the full, can be advantageous. An example of this is the traffic pattern in the Coombe. There is a long term possibility that Meath Street would become pedestrianised, because it is developing as a busy shopping area. Further, the heavy traffic on the Coombe suggests the need to eliminate some right hand turns by outgoing traffic. Ash street, which is largely residential, can be closed for this reason. It is proposed to do this and develop the end of Ash street, within the housing for this area, as a pedestrian route. By carefully integrating this element into new housing and by minor relocation, the spire of Pugin's church at John's lane lies on the axis of the pedestrian route. Further advantage is gained by concentrating social activities along this pedestrian route.

Existing Features of the Area

In preparing proposals for new residential development, the street patterns, the existing building forms on the site and adjacent to the site, together with the effect of buidings off site, such as factories, commercial buildings or churches, must be analysed. Existing buildings deemed essential for retention—for example large stone buildings, and viable shops with accommodation over them which could be rehabilitated, can and should be integrated with redevelopment.

The retention of large-scale buildings on the site helps to maintain a civic scale in new residential developments. The contrasting materials, as well as scale, combine with the new buildings to enliven the environment and provides a sense of orientation and identity with past community structures. The creation of new vistas along lines which will identify with existing church spires will also emphasise the continuity in the growth of the city and allow the traditional community to identify with historical and noteworthy landmarks.

Rehousing Without Relocation

In cases where redevelopment is not proposed, the rehabilitation of surviving or retained dwellings should be carried out for the people who live in them. It is illogical to remove a family from the area in which it developed, repair the vacated house and tenant that house with a new family. The result of this activity generally is that two families are rehoused, but both are socially disturbed, and the only gain is in administrative convenience.

Errors made in other countries in funding rehabilitation bear examination. These efforts have often resulted in subsidizing people who do not merit subsidization, e.g. speculators, and have failed to achieve the purpose of the subsidies, which is to help those in need.

By emphasising *people* therefore rather than *buildings*, and helping all who are in need to the extent of 100% funding for full rehabilitation (not partial), the aim of preserving the urban fabric and improving the housing stock will have been greatly advanced, and an equitable

9.8   Model of proposed low-rise redevelopment at the Coombe. NBA for Dublin Corporation

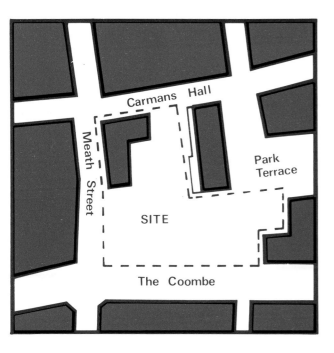

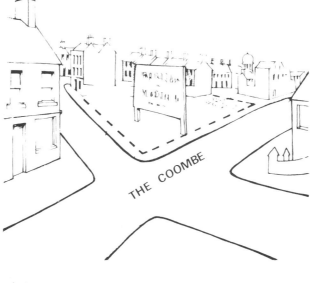

a) Area to be redeveloped

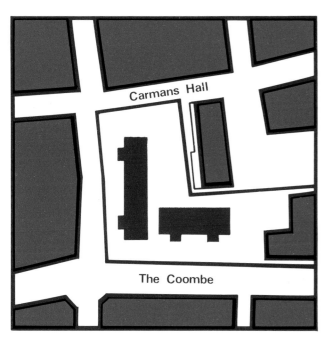

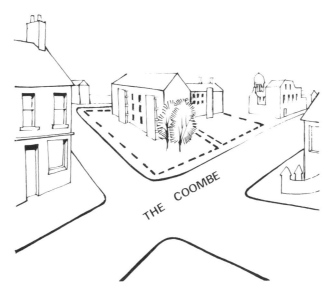

b) Solution ignoring urban structure

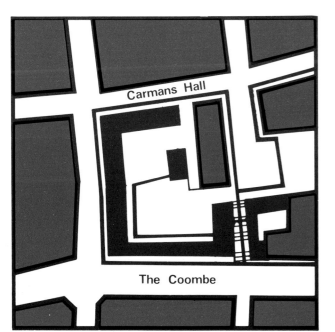

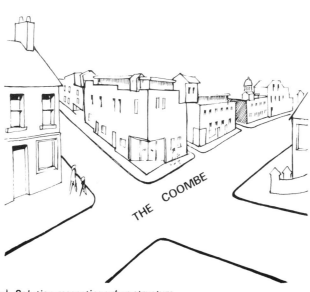

c) Solution respecting urban structure

distribution of the available funds will have been achieved. The possibility of linking the assessment of candidates for rehabilitation funding with social welfare assessments is one which self evidently commends itself to the authorities. The necessary legislation already exists.

Relationship to the Street

In respecting the pattern of existing streets, the precise relationship of the street to the dwelling becomes of major importance. Is the ground floor raised two or three steps above the pavement? Is there a small front garden? Is the porch recessed or projecting? Can raised pavements be used for added separation? Can houses be stepped vertically or horizontally? Considerable natural changes in level can be used to give access to upper storeys while maintaining contact with the ground, and this can be supplemented with further artificial cutting and filling of the ground, which is not uneconomical to shallow depths.

The proximity of a development area of the Coombe to the busy Meath street shopping area provides immediate contact with the bustle of city life. Integration with this bustle is satisfactorily achievable if the structure of the city is respected and any shortfalls made good.

The result, as shown on the sketch opposite, will be to preserve the street line and its life, and to create residential spaces which contrast with the street, as other spaces in the immediate area do.

The same sketch shows the damaging effect on the environment caused by redevelopment, which unfortunately, has become increasingly common in recent years. It is a building format which stops very far short of providing for the full needs of city life, and does nothing to improve the urban landscape.

Space About Buildings

by Andrew Devane

The Basic Component of Space

Space is defined as a "continuous extension viewed with or without reference to the existence of objects within it" or again as "interval between points or objects having, one or two, or three dimensions".

THE UNION OF SPACE AND STRUCTURE PROVIDES THE BASIC COMPONENT OF TOWNSCAPE.

Space in towns may be considered in two categories, both interdependent, both related to and generated by structure:

a) Surface space, e.g. — sites, open areas, roads;
b) Three-dimensional volumetic space, which encloses structures or is contained by them.

Aims

The aims of this case study are:—

To define the basic measure of Dublin — the unit of its framework, which is the individual site and its individual building, and to encourage study of the relationship of space and structure in the existing townscape of the city;

From the knowledge thus gained of the limitations imposed by the existing framework, to find ways of improving existing spaces and creating new ones in a positive, sensible and humane manner;

At every opportunity to appoint and use space — as one would building — as an essential and practical element in the revitalisation and enrichment of Dublin's urban and suburban matrix — nature and structure embedded in space;

To endeavour to resolve in some small way the crucial problems of spatial form and scale by analysing the familiar yet elusive measures of the many areas and elements which make our city what it is in eye and mind today — and which, whether we act or procrastinate, make it what it will be for the eyes and minds of the future.

The study ends with some examples of how space in existing and new situations has been handled, in the belief that deeds may speak louder than words.

Most architects have dealt with space — functionally and aesthetically — in designing specific buildings or areas; but few have had the opportunity of studying it in the context of urban planning and townscape, and fewer still of experiencing it and using it thus.

In small scale re-organisation of existing townscape, in the marriage of new structures or areas with existing ones the analysis and resolution of form and space are reasonably predictable. Failures here are sometimes due to a lack of understanding of the environment; more often, to a deliberate decision, whether idealistic or materialistic, to ignore or reject existing conditions as necessary design criteria.

Urban Space and Infill

The problems of infill and central city redevelopment, dealt with in other case studies, are inextricably enmeshed in urban space. No universal solutions are possible — each building, each development must be considered on its own merits in relation to its environment within a basic framework of enlightened by-laws — now long overdue — administered with discretion and understanding by a wise authority, dealing with architects whose primary responsibility in truth, beauty and code must be to the community at large rather than to any sectional interest.

In terms of Dublin's townscape, the fundamental problem to be resolved in each case is the extent to which the existing environment may condition the proposed development, and alternatively to what extent change may, with benefit, condition the existing — and future — environment. For better or for worse, fundamental propositions and decisions must be made in each case by planner and architect — sometimes agonisingly difficult decisions which relate to the whole unrealised concept and content of creative work on the one hand, and to the inescapable rights, realities and wrongs of the existing environment on the other.

There are no easy conclusions here; manifesto and dialectic wither in the bleak fields of reality, and the most beautiful and functional building in a wrong setting can become an urban nightmare.

However, the real difficulties occur in large-scale situations, e.g. instant plans for comprehensive urban redevelopment, with perhaps new infrastructure embedded into the existing city framework or tacked onto it. It is here that casual unions of structure and space can beget the most monstrous and unforeseen results, causing in turn permanent and dreadful damage to the existing and future townscape.

In sure hands, space can be as predictable and as definable as the structures related to it, even in large-scale developments; but too often in planning, space remains a two-dimensional drawingboard exercise — literally never getting off the ground, ignoring the third dimension.

Established Framework

It would be folly to discount the results and the lessons of the thousand years of life and growth we have inherited as a framework for our lives and times: a city of which a sizeable section is itself near death or is already dead. It is a framework over which we have — for good or ill — relatively limited powers for change or renewal, and for whose present parlous condition there can be no instant or universal remedy. Yet it is manifestly impossible to ignore or to replace in any major way the actual framework — streets, buildings, and spaces — of the city. Age and infirmity will not justify universal euthanasia, still less a programme of massive civic embalmment.

In such conditions, the study of existing conditions of two- and three-dimensional space in relation to structure, and in relation to the owner or user of that space, is urgently and fundamentally relevant.

One can consider Dublin in terms of two-dimensional space only, as an ancient yet ever-growing, ever-changing carpet with a mesh of roads binding a great pattern of individual sites and open spaces; a carpet spread — and spreading — in its topographical setting of river, plain, mountain and sea.

The main road pattern — the infrastructure space — is, generally speaking, already defined and set. Even allowing for essential future transport proposals, it is difficult now to foresee major changes save in a relatively small proportion of the present road system (although such changes as are proposed may cause great social and visual damage locally).

The existing streets vary in direction and width — anything from 40 to 150 feet between frontages; and it is the street space in relation to the height, mass

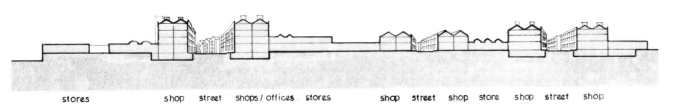

TYPICAL BUILT-UP CENTRAL CITY AREA.
Old back gardens filled in mainly with single storey shopping and stores, often with 100% site coverage.
Old service laneways have become secondary streets.
Average plot ratio approximately 2.0 : 1.

finish and details of the structure enclosing it which gives the city its definable character and scale.

The individual site, with its building pattern and its relation to other sites and to adjacent streets, merits closer study if for no other reason than that it was, is, and will for a long time remain, the fundamental unit of change. In Dublin the relationship of space to structure up to the present day follow well-established and definable principles and patterns, not only in the central area between the canals but in all parts of the city. (The few exceptions include some corporation flat developments.) But these relationships and densities vary greatly from area to area, period to period, street to street, building to building.

Historical plot ratios (the ratio of total floor area — basements excluded — to site area) vary from under 1 : 1 up to 1.5 - 1, seldom higher, except in central restricted built-up conditions. By comparison, in modern development, plot ratios of 2.5 : 1 and sometimes higher, have been permitted.

Need to review present policies
Present thinking on plot ratio (and on site densities likewise) needs reviewing, in the light of many factors, e.g. the economic situation; land availability and land values; building-heights and zoning; above all, the effects of the present and future energy situation on the siting and servicing of buildings. *It would appear that a good case can be made for reduced plot ratios in certain sectors; little can be said for increasing them, even in central areas.*

Dublin sites are normally rectangular — even in the old city — short side to street, varying in size from 13 feet frontage by less than 30 feet deep for little 'back to back' houses, to over 50 feet frontage by 300 feet deep for some of the greater georgian houses, and the large inner-suburb houses. The dimensions of a central area site might be averaged at about 22 feet frontage by 100 feet or more in depth, although the range in variety is very great. While the sites may vary in size the building pattern occupying them has been basically the same whatever the period or style. The depth as

often conditions the road pattern as it is conditioned by it.

In the central area the buildings were usually terraced, being one to five stories over ground level (five being at or just beyond the tolerable limit prior to the era of the elevator). They were almost invariably set back from the pavement by a front 'area' which gave light, air and access to the basement, or alternatively in the smaller houses, by a front garden. On the larger sites the main building fronting the street was anything from 30 feet to 50 feet deep — and was often extended farther to the rear by a return building, generally two stories over ground level and often projecting 40 feet or more into the back garden, occupying one-third to half of its width.

Sometimes these return buildings were built back to back, but oftener not, as they depended for access on the main stair landings and these in turn depended on the position of the street entrance. Paired entrances are less common until recently.

The average inner area back garden stretched a further 50 to 150 feet from the rear main house to the almost universal coach house at the end. This was generally a two-storey terraced structure running the full width of the garden by 20 feet to 40 feet deep and almost invariably backing on to a service laneway, or on to a private yard opening on to that laneway. In the older areas, service lanes have often been eliminated in the passage of time, and they are rarely provided in newer developments. The diagrams show some of the more commonly recurring combinations of space structure.

Descriptions of this familiar almost standard layout would be completely superfluous were it not for the fact that, applied to sites of varying sizes and to different periods, it provides Dublin with its basic unit — its basic matrix of space and structure. Despite certain shortcomings, the arrangement has worked well, and has had a remarkable flexibility and variety in terms of use and expansion, one on which it is exceedingly difficult to improve. Original dwelling-houses and sites have been converted, individually and collectively and with singular success, into shops, offices, hotels, hospitals, apartments and tenements (these for all their squalor, could still teach us much in terms of social needs and community planning). Former gardens have become sites for meeting rooms, dance halls, theatres, cinemas, factories, garages, warehouses and a great range of commercial and processing areas — all with remarkably little physical change and the minimum of mechanical aids or technology. Coach houses and mews yards still shelter many workshops and businesses as well as providing residential accommodation in some areas.

Most of this has been contained within the spaces and structures of an aged framework, much of it built 150 years and more, much of it physically unsound, and much no longer capable of further change or improvement in any reasonable or practical manner if the standards and requirements of our times are to be complied with; standards and requirements which, it should be noted, are anything but absolute in these days of change.

While in many instances it will be quite possible to maintain and use sections of this framework in a practical and economical way for quite some time to come, it would be completely unrealistic to imagine that preservation can be applied as a sensible and

LARGER SITES - CENTRAL CITY AREA.

Street dominent with established quality and character.
Large quantity open space still present.
Average plot ratio 1·1:1

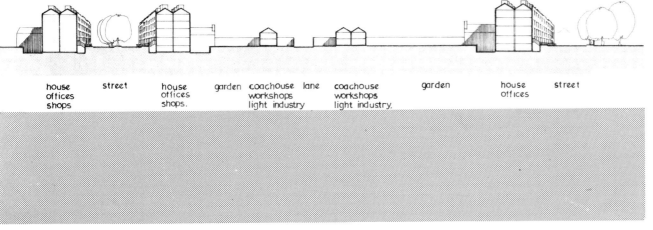

| house offices shops | street | house offices shops. | garden | coachouse lane workshops light industry | coachouse workshops light industry. | garden | house offices | street |

universal solution to Dublin's present and future problems.

There can be no doubt that there is an absolute obligation to preserve at all costs certain buildings and certain limited precincts as living entities — or even at worst, as museum pieces or places, if there be no other reasonable and effective way of maintaining them for posterity. "At all costs" means at cost to us all, for they are inescapably our individual civic and national responsibility, which must be honoured now and for all time.

The preserved and the unpreservable

But what of the remainder of the infirm framework, the spaces and the structures, the streets and the precincts? They cannot be preserved; they will not last indefinitely. What is to become of whole areas of our city in use and content, in time? Are they to be maintained or retained beyond reason — or left as wastelands — or rebuilt in wretched facsimile of an unattainable past? Or are they to be dismembered in large or small pieces, and be rebuilt in the style of the hour — site by site, street by street — on the basis that content and form follow function and that all will be well in time? Can we visualise an interim development period, full of boundless variety, with inevitably strained relationships between styles and the existing environment — or perhaps no relationships at all? Can the unity and the quality of the street and the square — the space enclosed by the structures — be retained without preserving the structures themselves?

The following factors emerge from any consideration of the existing space structure framework:

> Firstly, the surprising extent of the space which is still un-built and under-built, both in individual sites and in cleared areas in the city. In terms of available space, there would appear to be little justification for any overall increase in density in central areas. What is required is planned development within the norms and disciplines of the existing framework.

> Secondly, the visual and social importance, in terms of space structure and people, of the street as the controlling factor in regeneration and redevelopment. The principle of the street — its quality and its character — must remain paramount, whether it be in the plans for a single site or for the whole city. If Dublin is to remain alive visually, the street in general terms must be maintained, fostered, developed as an entity of parts — as part of the whole. This does not mean physical preservation — although in certain areas preservation is necessary. It *does* mean conservation and development of the quality and character of the street if these exist, their creation where there is neither. It makes formidable demands on the understanding, excellence, and humility, of architect and artist, each battling with his individual problems in the context of his beliefs, work and time. There are no overall solutions here — only a great deal of labour and agony with relatively little hope of complete success. If the site is the measure of the city, the street *is* the city, and is the generator of its future.

Some specific examples

Examples follow of how problems of space related to structures in different contexts and in different environments have been handled. These are not presented as ideal or universal solutions, merely as examples of attempts to apply the above principles to individual situations.

In considering examples we should consider space — two- and three-dimensional space — in its various other relationships — especially with nature. In more ways than one, exterior space is the city dweller's quotient of nature, his window of the seasons, yard-stick of the elements. As density increases and crushes space, nature recedes until, as in downtown New York, it virtually disappears, dominated and supplanted by structures and technology gone mad, and one commences to live in a sub-nature world.

The use of nature, of plant forms alive and growing within man-made space, provides a great potential as yet virtually untapped in Dublin; a potential least often used in the areas of greatest need — e.g., the derelict sites and the bleak transition areas.

Importance of Landscaping

The application of landscaping, even in a temporary fashion, to fill or bridge gaps between old and new would give great rewards for relatively small outlay; buildings and townscape — or the lack of them — softened, scaled, defined, dissolved by nature.

If the Liffey — from Butt bridge to Guinness's brewery — were lined with trees and shrubs planted on the existing paths (with perhaps new paths cantilevered a little lower over the river, combined with our long-awaited clear, tide-free Liffey water !) how the riverside dereliction and decay and the traumatic time of transition could be softened and screened, with the creation of a gentle new environment where one could walk again, and look at the river and its reflections, as we did long ago, without seeing too much beyond it ! Or again, why not more bold tree-forms in central O'Connell street — barbarously bereft of Nelson — or similar trees in Dorset street, changing the scale, outlook and amenities on one of the city's main and most dreary approaches for the delight not only of its visitors but also for that of its own inhabitants.

The only universally valid principle is that the spaces about, between and within buildings, must be designed — in three-dimensions, in harmony and scale with the buildings — just as those buildings must relate to one another and to their neighbours. Within the frame-work, each case is a special case, and requires active design. Too often in the past, "open space" has meant that part of the site left over after the buildings have been placed on it. This situation must change; only then shall all be well "and

All manner of things shall be well
When the tongues of flame are in-folded
Into the crowned knot of fire
And the fire and the rose are one."

Above all, spaces must have natural living and growing elements within them. Nature, gently handled, will not fail us. For every consideration we show her in our city, she will (men willing) repay a thousandfold.

Large Urban High Density Mixed Development (Irish Life Centre, Abbey Street)

Site about 4½ acres in run-down area of near-derelict buildings fronting lower Abbey street, Gardiner street and Talbot street, and bounded on its south eastern corner by the loop line railway bridge. Plot ratio 2.5 : 1.

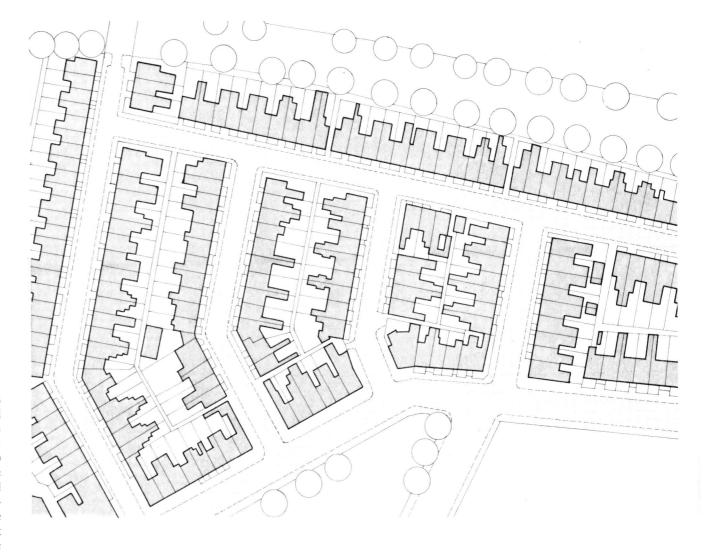

house yard lane yard house road house yard lane yard house road house lane house road house lane
SINGLE STOREY RESIDENTIAL

road garden house garden store lane store garden house road house garden store lane store garden house garden
TWO STOREY RESIDENTIAL.

TYPICAL INNER SUBURBS - 18 th. and 19 th. CENTURY.

High street to site ratio.
Much light and sky, - limited trees and shrubs. Great potential for improvement within the existing framework, with mixed residential and planned community facilities.
Character and dominance of streets vary considerably in these areas.
Plot ratio approximately   0·5:1 · single storey
                            0·7:1 · 2 - storey

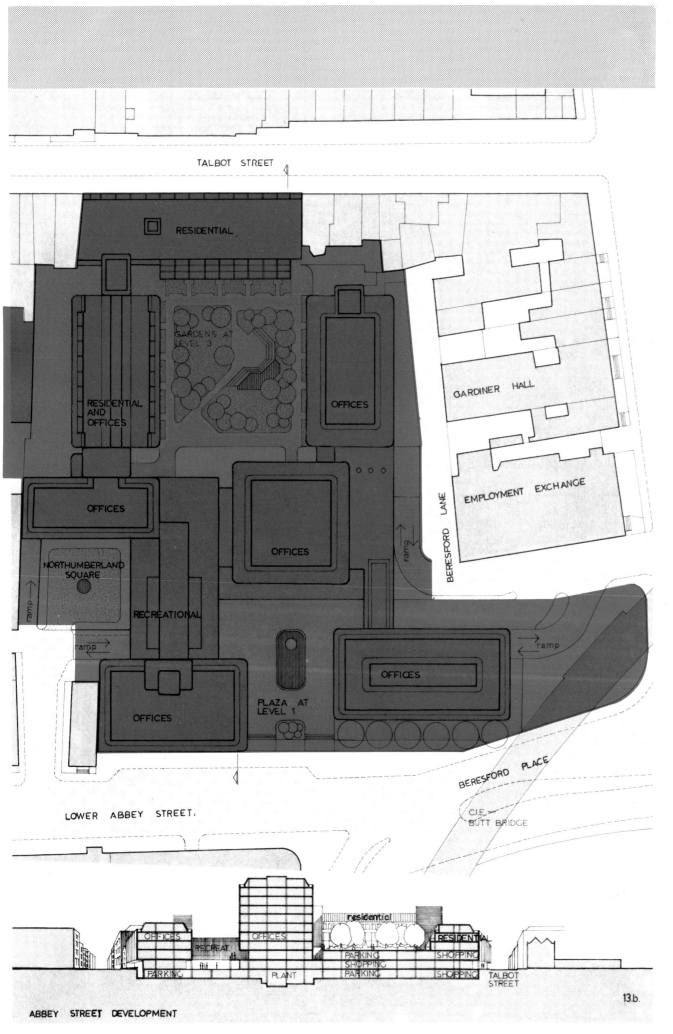

TALBOT STREET

RESIDENTIAL

GARDENS AT LEVEL 3

RESIDENTIAL AND OFFICES

OFFICES

GARDINER HALL

OFFICES

EMPLOYMENT EXCHANGE

BERESFORD LANE

OFFICES

NORTHUMBERLAND SQUARE

OFFICES

ramp

RECREATIONAL

ramp

ramp

OFFICES

OFFICES

PLAZA AT LEVEL 1

BERESFORD PLACE

LOWER ABBEY STREET.

C.I.E. BUTT BRIDGE

OFFICES RECREAT OFFICES residential RESIDENTIAL

PARKING PARKING SHOPPING TALBOT STREET

PARKING PLANT PARKING SHOPPING

13.b.

ABBEY STREET DEVELOPMENT

The street form is being maintained, enclosed and developed with buildings which are related to it in mass and scale and finish, aimed at achieving a balance whether the railway bridge is ultimately retained or removed. Decisions in respect of the bridge and other surrounding areas are still to be made.

Abbey street and Butt bridge extension open into a plaza which serves as pedestrian access to buildings of various heights grouped around it and the adjoining Northumberland square. This in turn leads by arcade to Talbot street. These spaces aim to create within themselves and as seen from the street, a new utilitarian amenity for the general public as well as for those occupying the first level of the complex.

As this is the first major scheme in Dublin to incorporate residential accommodation with shopping, offices, and recreational facilities, and as the surrounding environment is dreary, and noisy with traffic and trains, a large landscaped garden with mature trees surrounded by residential recreational and office buildings of varying heights is set at the heart of the complex at the third level, above the shopping and parking areas, to provide what is hoped will be a homely and peaceful haven for the use of the occupants and their friends.

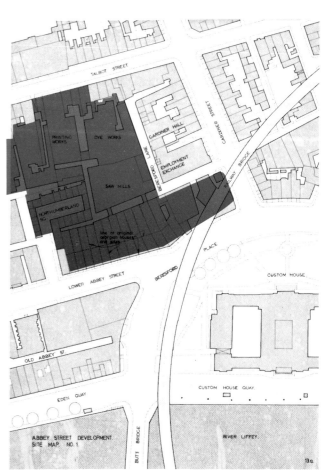

TALBOT STREET

GARDINER HALL

GARDINER STREET

PRINTING WORKS

DYE WORKS

BERESFORD LANE

EMPLOYMENT EXCHANGE

SAW MILLS

NORTHUMBERLAND SQ.

BERESFORD PLACE

CUSTOM HOUSE

LOWER ABBEY STREET

OLD ABBEY ST.

EDEN QUAY

CUSTOM HOUSE QUAY

ABBEY STREET DEVELOPMENT SITE MAP NO. 1

BUTT BRIDGE

RIVER LIFFEY

13a.

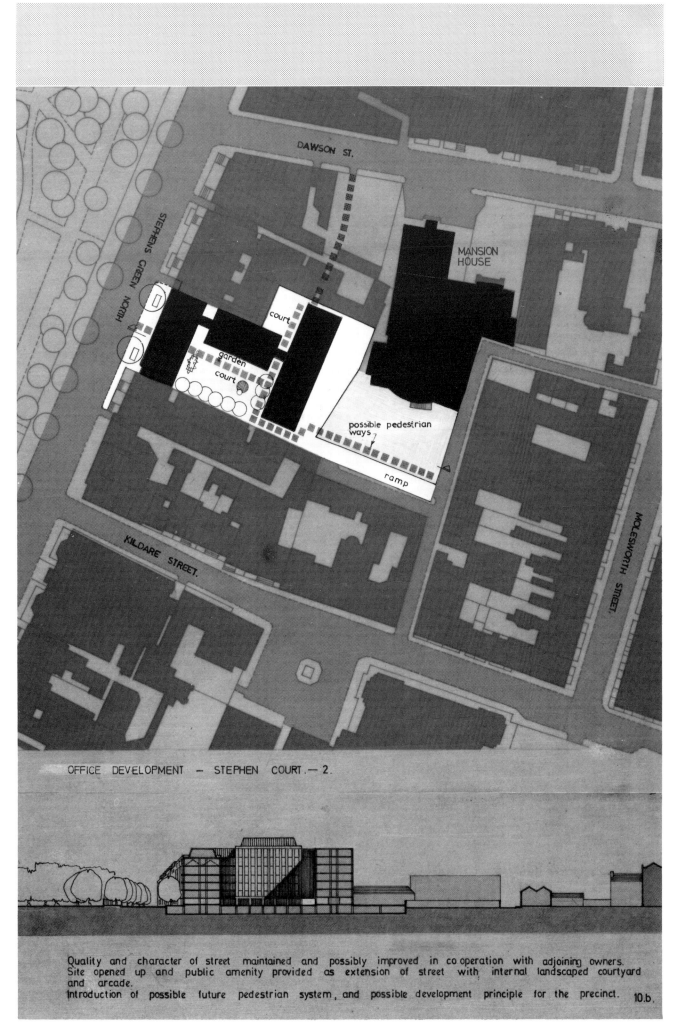

DAWSON ST.

MANSION HOUSE

STEPHENS GREEN NORTH

court

garden court

possible pedestrian ways

ramp

KILDARE STREET.

MOLESWORTH STREET.

OFFICE DEVELOPMENT — STEPHEN COURT. — 2.

Quality and character of street maintained and possibly improved in co operation with adjoining owners. Site opened up and public amenity provided as extension of street with internal landscaped courtyard and arcade.
Introduction of possible future pedestrian system, and possible development principle for the precinct. 10.b.

10.10 Stephen's Court—exterior

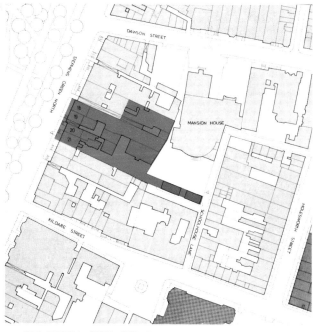

OFFICE DEVELOPMENT — STEPHEN COURT — 1

Large built-over site at back of 4 georgian houses (3 very indifferent and unaligned).
Sited between two ranges of magnificent georgian houses, nos. 14 to 17, and nos. 22 to 23.
Conservation of facades and street of great importance.

Large Suburban Low Density Mixed Development (A.I.B. Headquarters, Ballsbridge)

The large site fronts the Royal Dublin Society's headquarters and is flanked by Irish Hospitals Sweepstakes buildings on one side, by residential development on the other, and at the rear runs the railway. The complex comprises low-rise unit offices embedded in landscaped parkland, stepped, linked and related in height and scale to R.D.S. and the residential surroundings.

The completed project will contain Educational Centre, with trainees residence for 90 people, recreation centre, computer centre (all linked to underground carparking and service areas), and to blocks of flats containing a total of 90 residential units. Also provided are main stores and printing works. Plot ratio — less than 1 : 1.

In this case the street is contained and enriched by landscaping and buildings on Merrion road and by road widening, planting and buildings on Serpentine avenue. No attempt is made to change the character or scale of the neighbourhood spatially — merely to enhance it with nature on buildings and in parkland.

10.6   New A.I.B. headquarters, Ballsbridge

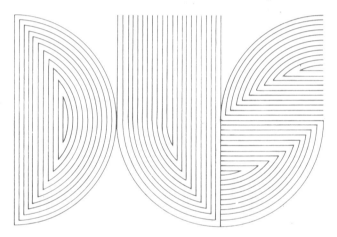

Parkland and Suburban Neighbourhood Development (Rathfarnham Village)

This is an example of the development of a large private open space scaled and related to the village street and to the surrounding residential environment.

The site —over 50 acres — adjoins the single street village of Rathfarnham, and encloses Rathfarnham Castle, and adjoining buildings. Lack of parking, and the building of a new road as originally proposed by Dublin Corporation, would almost certainly have ended the commercial life of the village.

A scheme was prepared with one basic principle — that of responsible development — one in which people and their environment were more important than maximum profit. The principal aims were the survival and revitalisation of the village with a small increase in shopping developed as an extension of the main street, and the creation of a mixed residential and neighbourhood development for a balanced community, rather than a single-class ghetto.

The mass and scale of the castle, the proposed recreational buildings, the low level office development and trees form the spine of development in relation to the (ultimately) tree-lined dual carriageway to the west, with the low profile of the village beyond it and the decreasing height and density of the residential area to the east.

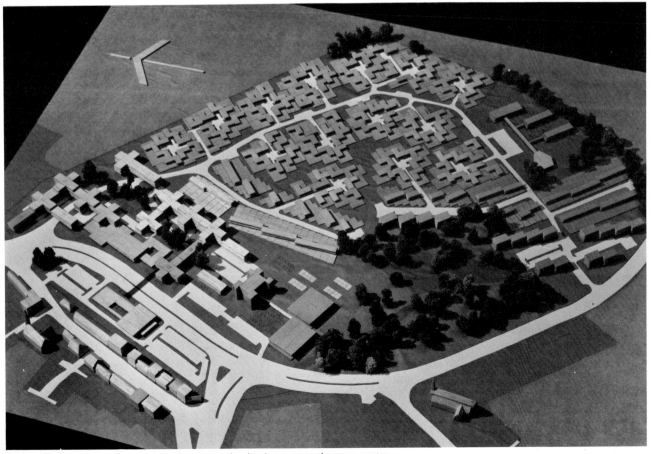

10.7   Rathfarnham village and castle—proposed redevelopment at the town centre

Suburbs and Outskirts

Buildings in
Established Landscape
by Raymond MacDonnell

Open Space
in New Housing
by James Fehily

Suburban Infill

by Patrick Rooney

11.01

Buildings in Established Landscape

by Raymond MacDonnell

The Tradition

House design in Ireland has two traditional poles — the thatched cottage built with mud or stone walls, and the georgian terraced house. Both are valid architectural forms using largely indigenous materials; in both cases due to the limiting factor of available materials, unity of architectural expression was manifested; in one by the similar scale of all the cottages with their white lime-washed walls, straw coloured thatched roofs, small windows and half-doors, all in perfect harmony, producing one of the most famous vernacular styles in the world.

In the other, the georgian terraced house, the limiting factors were deliberately imposed — standardised windows, door designs, railings and fireplaces, all varying in subtle sophisticated ways, but generally using the same colour bricks and the same building heights, planned around a landscaped open space or park.

Today there is hardly any equivalent to match the standard of these particular styles; instead, we have a predominance of ribbon-developed, semi-detached houses of dreadful design, with built-in duality. From an endless variety of materials now available we have not produced anything to approach the vernacular Irish thatched cottage or the georgian house. We have a multiplicity of so-called "styles" fighting with each other visually. The lack of either self-control on the part of the developers or control externally exposed has resulted in monotonous rows of houses around our towns, mean in scale and devoid of order.

This article illustrates how housing "built in scenery", or built where there was scenery before the houses were planned, can be handled.

Market Forces

The combination of indifference on the part of the house-buying public, the speculative builder-developer (the prime mover in the provision of private sector housing) and our unimaginative planning regulations has resulted in the present scene, which is not without character though not a very attractive one and certainly seldom beautiful. It is distinctive, and quite different from continental housing and although it has some similarities with British housing examples, it differs also from these.

In the field of two-storey housing, this difference is mainly manifested in the choice of building materials rather than in the architectural form which varies from housing in Britain only in detail, arising from the urge to combine diverse building materials in different manners. The indigenous concrete block, plastered, possibly with a brick front up to the first floor is typical of the period when burnt-clay bricks became scarce and labour more expensive in the Dublin area from the '30s to the '50s. Now, with the ready availability of concrete bricks and the exploitation of new brick-clay deposits, combined with a period of greater affluence, and the all-brick house is creeping back into the outer Dublin surburban scene.

The housing which has been erected in the outer ring of Dublin in recent years, built generally by the speculative developer, is a fair expression of the level of architectural consciousness of our people during this particular period. The speculative builder only builds what he thinks he can sell. The lack of sophistication in the design types, the almost complete lack of regard for the preservation of trees, and the total absence of a demand, on the part of the buying public, for proper orientation and the preservation of views by good planning, at least until very recently, truly expresses our indifference, whether or not we like to admit this.

When we examine the one-off-houses, which are often either grouped too closely or set too far apart, we see the character of the Dublin middle class of the '60s and '70s. Due to the unfortunate land speculations of recent years, with resultant high land-costs, the builder has been forced to put houses, the sizes and scales of which would suit half-acre sites, choc-a-block on lots 40' or 50' wide. The result is comparatively large 2,000 sq. ft. houses with pitched gable roofs adjoining flat roofs, adjoining hipped roofs, bungalows adjoining two-storey houses with apparently no objections from the local authorities. This chaos seems to pervade the world of private house building at present. It is the permissive age of architecture, producing uncontrolled visual violence. Gone is the sense of order which informed earlier generations. There is little self-control; hence the conglomerations and glut of materials employed without any real knowledge of the true functions of these materials.

Editor's Note: The pictures in this article illustrate, as the author emphasises, the importance of respect for existing landscape and the addition of new landscaping elements in housing developments; those in the two articles which follow concentrate more on the consequences of ignoring such essential procedures. The moral in both cases is the same.

11.02

11.03

11.04

11.05

Building regulations, where they require that all drains and pipes be kept on external walls, have resulted in spaghetti-like horrors all over the rear elevations, thus making the back of the average house ugly in the extreme, even where, on the front, some small amount of control has been exercised — to " put on a good front". The insistence that bathroom and w.c.s be located at external walls has, of course, influenced the elevations and the resultant smaller windows, with their obscured glass, seldom relate proportionately well to other rear windows. We see here, also, that the components available (again controlled by the demand) often result in symmetrical windows being used in asymmetrical facades.

The planning of estates has generally, to date, been carried out with a total disregard for orientation. The indifference on the part of the buyer, who has accepted this situation, has therefore left the way open for unscrupulous developers, who have employed pliant architects to prepare estate layouts where the only criterion was the number of houses that could be got on a site; and then sold their approved sites to a third man — the builder — who knew that, until recently, he could sell virtually anything, regardless of quality.

The consequence has been a succession of layouts produced straight from ordnance maps, with a few contours of levels added sufficient to sales by the local authority. Once approved, such a layout made it impossible for the second architect, if one were even appointed, to do anything with the development; unless the builder-client was a philanthrophist, who was prepared to wait a further period for a fresh planning permission (not to mention the time needed to revise the design). If the only saying ' Architecture is an expression of the culture of an age ' is true, we are indeed now in rather a poor state.

Unimaginative and Rigid Control

From the planning point of view, many arbitrary rules, e.g. insistence on a 35′ minimum back garden rather than on a respect for privacy and each case being examined on its own merits, has resulted in 83

11.06

11.07

11.08

shoddy and featureless development. Rigid application of standard building limits and minimum set-backs which become maxima, and the uncritical application of standard widths of roads, verges and footpaths, regardless of the status and function of the particular road, have contributed to the dire monotony of the end product.

Another aspect of development control which must be tackled at local authority level is the despoilment of the existing scenery surrounding villages on the outskirts of the city. Instead of insisting that the villages be expanded directly from the core, planning permission for bungalows on 70′ minimum lots, has resulted in the most dreadful honky-tonk ribbon developments, radiating outwards from a neglected village core. Coupled with this has been the ever-increasing spread of the city suburbs, cutting through some of these villages, swallowing them up and destroying their character, creating new centres and nodes, without any regard for the old traditional centres (usually around a church) and making no effort to renew, or make good, existing buildings worthy of preservation.

More Action Plans Needed

Proper total planning of districts by means of agreed Action Plans could ensure the retention of existing well-planted areas of scenic value as parks and playing areas. Instead of each developer providing a fixed proportion of open space within his own site, the local authority should do so, and pay for the reserved sites at housing land market value, out of a pro-rata levy on all developers in the area. This method of securing a proper pattern and hierarchy of open spaces is already written into existing development plans; but it requires to be actively implemented.

11.09

11.10

Open Space in New Housing

by James Fehily

The Controversy

Open space in new housing has now become one of the most topical and controversial issues to occupy alike the columns of newspapers and the programmes of professional seminars. Most correspondence and discussion has tended to confuse rather than enlighten; a situation hardly surprising, since the subject is now a target for theorists in fields which in many cases would appear to be far removed from the day-to-day struggle of the industry to provide adequate housing. Criminologists, sociologists, community organisers, recreation experts, politicians and priests — all can find explanations of current social problems in the unsatisfactory way which developers provide open space in new housing estates. The complaints are many and varied — insufficient open space, space in the wrong place, bleak and ugly space, inadequate recreation facilities, poor design, bad ground conditions, lack of supervision and maintenance.

These complaints seem valid, and a glance around us will show that many are so; but on closer examination, others will be found to be in mutual conflict, or to be irreconcilable with current economic conditions or the individual preferences of residents. A short study cannot hope to suggest acceptable solutions to all of these problems; but it would at least be useful to identify the various organisations which participate in housing development, and the problems which must be solved, if pleasant and enjoyable open spaces are to be a reality. Housing can be carried out either by local authorities or commercial developers and, while the primary objectives are not identical, the procedure is the same, and so the distinction can be ignored in the present context.

Site Selection

The first requirement is obviously the selection of a site with physical characteristics conducive to a good end product — mature trees, moderate undulation in ground form, pleasant views, streams and, above all, good well-drained soil. These characteristics have rarely been a priority in the selection of sites for housing development, and valid criticism of past and current practice can be made on this basis.

With the exception of old estates and large private gardens, the Irish countryside consists largely of fields bounded by scrub hedges with intermittent ash, elm or sycamore, growing on an earth bank formed from an adjoining drainage ditch.

The vegetation is usually old, scraggy, and rarely of a quality compatible with new high density housing; while the earth banks create problems in retaining trees, because of discrepancy in ground levels. The water flow in the ditches varies with rainfall, and for long periods they can be dry, or (more likely) muddy receptacles for junk and rubbish, a problem which gets worse with increased population, and which in turn generates a demand for culverting or infill. Between the hedges are bleak open spaces which have been cleared of trees to facilitate cultivation.

However, despite these disadvantages, a great deal can be achieved through sensitive selection of sites and a positive attitude to potential resources. Small local authorities obviously have a wider range of choice when it comes to site selection than the large urban authorities, which unfortunately have greatest need. In the Dublin region especially, land is more expensive and choice is more restricted because of the need to link new development with large-scale drainage systems. Conversely, however, comprehensive zoning and detailed action plans should facilitate greater freedom in locating building and open space in the areas best suited to each.

Public Attitudes

Apart from the problems of land, there are also the problems of attitudes in the political sector. Rightly or wrongly, elected representatives too often give the impression of being concerned solely with quantity of houses rather than with quality of housing, statements to the contrary being generally regarded as verbal deflections of criticism from effete minority groups. Officials tend to say that improved environment can only result from sustained pressure by community groups directly applied to the politicians; meanwhile the politicians say that, despite appearances, decision-making is effectively restricted to the civil service and the Minister.

Further to confuse the angry residents, the blame for failure is also distributed evenly between the planner, developer, architect and contractor; and in the end, the uninformed observer has no idea where the buck actually stops. While officials both technical and administrative may have limited power, they do in fact have a great deal of influence; but the effectiveness of technical officers appear to have been steadily eroded during the last ten years. There are many reasons for this change, but the following are probably the more important: During the relative boom of the '60s, the local authorities found it extremely difficult to recruit experienced and competent technical staff; responsibility became diffused through a proliferation of semi-state organisations, all involved in physical development; technicians with limited training began to claim competence in all related fields, although these claims were not often sustained in practice.

Possibly even more damaging to prestige and self-confidence was the increasingly brutal pressure which bureaucracy was subjected to by amateur groups and advocates of "participation", few of whom took the trouble to analyse critically the degree of knowledge and application which would be required from themselves if their participation in planning were to have any meaning.

Last, and possibly the most destructive influence, has been the prolonged orgy of self-criticism which has characterised the planning professions in recent years. This has opened the gates to a flood of superficial media comment, which in turn has confused the public and destroyed confidence in professional planning. The nett result has been increasing reluctance on the part of professional people in public service to make decisions, which are an essential part of their jobs, and to be publicly identified with those decisions.

In the interests of tangible progress in the immediate future, it would be helpful if the local authority planning professionals would consider the following suggestions:—

1. To ignore for the moment the wilder and usually untried theories on community planning which increasingly pour in from across the Atlantic and the Irish Sea.

2. To spell out clearly the factual limitations in relation to land, finance and management, so that these limitations are crystal-clear to all concerned.

12.1   Typical "raw" material for housing

85

12.2　Finglas—not a tree in sight

3.　To evolve criteria for density and site development which are compatible with these limitations while meeting common-sense needs for private and public space, traffic circulation, recreation and relaxation. In evolving these criteria, there must be effective input from landscape architects and park managers if the present imbalance between structures, hard materials and roads on the one hand and living greenery on the other is to be corrected.

4.　To insist that development plans maximise existing site assets in the preparation of layouts, and also ensure the preservation of these assets in the development process.

5.　To ensure full implementation of open space development on completion of the project.

6.　To provide for adequate and continuing management of the project, either through public resources, or through community effort.

The Professions

Traditionally, landscape architecture has been regarded as a terminal skill in the housing process, limited to advice on the choice and location of trees and shrubs after the positions of buildings, roads and services have been fixed; but by the time all of these hazards have been avoided, the few areas left where trees can be planted rarely have much relevance to the spatial organisation of the scheme. Ideally that skill should be available to the housing designer, not merely from the initial planning stage, but even from the earlier stage of site-selection and evaluation.

Architecture and landscape, although related, have quite distinct design priorities: the landscape architect appraises the whole site, in which buildings, ground forms, tree masses, edges and views are all equally important in putting together the finished product. There is also a definite hierarchy in the design process, so that secondary elements, such as vehicle circulation, parking and services are not permitted to dictate the final form, but are allocated their appropriate role in the scheme. Perhaps the most severe criticism of current new building is the insensitivity to context. Large new structures stand in crude juxtaposition to older ones, without respect for scale, form, material or colour; existing ground forms, which with perception and imaginative integration could blend new buildings with existing landscapes, are flattened to facilitate easy planning and construction; the potential of valuable existing trees as form-elements in the final composition is not realised, and usually end up in impossible positions, both vertically and horizontally, and as a consequence, rarely survive.

Apart from aesthetic considerations, the existing lack of knowledge on the part of most architects and engineers in relation to soils, drainage and vegetation in general, must inevitably contribute to the low standard of development in new housing. Architectural and engineering training, over the years, has been mainly responsible for these attitudes: the educational programme deals with elements and materials which can be finitely fixed in shape to accurately predetermined forms, and consequently there is an antipathy to elements and materials which have a life of their own, which change seasonally and throughout the years and which do not respond in the same precise way as concrete to shuttering or bricks to the mould. Hence, during recent years, in the U.S. and Britain, there has been an over obsession with vast paved areas, devoid of vegetation, while the Swiss have maintained their unique capacities to produce beautifully balanced designs combining hard and soft materials in just the right proportions. These schemes are obviously a product of designers whose training and experience have developed an equal understanding of both materials.

The irony of all this is that there are few architects, planners or engineers, who do not respond enthusiastically to a skilfully and richly landscaped development; but where this happens, they tend to feel it happens naturally, and they have considerable difficulty recognising the skill involved, or in integrating it with their own specific skills. It is equally unfortunate that many landscape architects have little understanding of, or sympathy for, modern architecture, conceiving it as something to be hidden, that only trees can make a place. The public, however, suffer no confusion on this

12.4　American hard landscaping

12.3　Housing well set amongst existing trees

12.5　Swiss hard and soft landscape

point. Attractively landscaped housing estates are at a premium on the market, and attractive properties always fetch a higher price.

Specifically, a professionally-landscaped housing estate will have a deliberately complementary relationship between planting and earthforms on the one hand, and building layout on the other. Circulation systems are organised at different scales and, as in a well designed building, form tangible spatial sequences. Trees and shrubs are selected and located to provide the character for each space, and the form of the space reflects the activity. The changes due to seasons are foreseen, and are deliberately provided for; as are also soil conditions, drainage, public use, and future management.

Contractors

Imprecise specifications and inadequate penalties for default make it easy for contractors to evade their responsibilities for adequate site management. The three main areas of failure are:— destruction of existing trees, destruction of top-soil, and destruction of completed landscape work by other trades. Assuming goodwill on the part of the contractor, most of these difficulties can be resolved by clear and detailed discussion at the beginning of the job, which of course implies that landscape must be integrated at the start of the project. The issue which leads to greatest contention between the general contractor and the landscape contractor concerns the condition of the site on handover; few specifications ever clarify what this condition should be, and consequently there are arguments, delays and claims either by the landscape contractor or the house owner. Finally, there is the problem of initial maintenance between the time the landscape contractor leaves the site and the owner or local authority takes over; many good schemes have been spoiled, and a lot of money has been wasted, in the absence of provision for this service.

Residents

Ultimately, the quality of the neighbourhood will depend largely on the residents, who are the most difficult group in the process to organise; all the others are identifiable at an early stage and can be co-ordinated or pressured if necessary. Many residents in new communities still come from rural backgrounds, where densities are so low and Nature so predominant that damage or neglect on the part of the individual makes little impact. This situation is largely the result of regarding land as a source from which income can be extracted and not as the material for a pleasant environment. When this attitude is transferred to a high density situation with few soft areas, the consequences are disastrous. Ignorance is also a problem; knowledge of trees is usually confined to knowing which one makes a good fire. Personal values are another problem; the urge to identify each property clearly, regardless of context, the obsession with detached and semi-detached houses, vulgarity in taste, the demand for car access at both ends of the property when combined with on-site parking, result in 80% of the areas exposed to public view being hard surfaced.

Another problem is the difference in public attitudes towards privately owned and rented houses; in the absence of good management, rented properties are synonymous with poor maintenance. Finally, there is a lack of tradition of co-operative effort. Elsewhere, local authorities have tackled these problems in various ways with considerable success. The professional design and planting of one garden in a housing group has a

12.6   Nowhere to play

12.7   Somewhere to play

12.9   A haven for the pedestrian

12.8   Amsterdam: canal converted to park

major influence on the other residents; the same effect is also obtained by a high standard of landscape around public buildings, e.g. school, church, shopping centre, etc.

Standards

Discussion of standards is usually confined to arguments concerning the precise area of land which should be allocated as open space in any particular development: apart from playing pitches and tennis courts, which cannot be used unless they conform to specific dimensions, the issue for discussion is quality and not quantity. If parks are to be attractive, they must be designed to provide a variety of spaces for different uses linked together by paths from which there are changing vistas and views as the public move about. Ugly surroundings should be screened out; sitting areas should be protected from wind, face the sun, and overlook planting which is interesting and pleasant throughout the year. Children's play should be close, but separate; traffic movement and noise should be insulated, and the ubiquitous playing-field kept well out of sight. One acre of well designed, well maintained park will give more pleasure than ten acres of bare, windswept, open space. A comparison between Palmerston park and Ringsend park clearly illustrates this point.

Real Participation

The use of demonstration plots in the main public space to show the range of plants available, and how they can be arranged, has been very successful at Craigavon new town. Whatever method is employed, however, the lead must come from the local authority. In relation to co-operative effort, which will become more and more essential as public resources diminish, the experience of Bord Failte in the Tidy Towns programme is very relevant:—

> They have found new communities extremely difficult to organise; in fact, in only one case have they been successful; usually they have to wait until residents' associations are formed for other purposes and then work through them:

> Normally there must be some strong personality in the community who will organise the other residents and through whom the public agency must act:

> Small communities are invariably more successful than large, and this is very relevant to the basic development plan, which should facilitate the evolution of close-knit community groups:

> Prizes for performance are a valuable incentive, but not essential:

> and, finally, (most interesting but not entirely surprising discovery) co-operative action decreases as affluence increases.

Many of the residents' problems have more to do with sociology and education than with professional planning, but it is suggested that many practical steps can be taken to improve the situation:—

1. Physical layouts which are conducive to the formation of small community groups.

2. Competent and integrated professional design for the appropriate areas in the scheme.

3. Organised management with facilities aimed at integrating new members of communities, until the communities themselves take over.

4. An educational input on schools which would provide a knowledge of plants and the physical environment possibly in the currently nebulous civics course.

5. Prizes and penalties(?) for good or bad maintenance of personal property.

6. A competent Tenants' or Residents' Advisory Service.

7. Less public emphasis on the responsibilities of the State and Society, and more emphasis on action by individuals and individual communities.

12.10   "Personalised" housing

12.11   The importance of orientation

12.12   Irish hard and soft landscaping

12.13   Even a few trees can be important

12.14   Quality and maintenance matter more than percentage of open space.

Suburban Infill

by Patrick Rooney

DEFINITION
The word suburban means:
of, in or like a suburb — conventional — petty —
a suburb, part of outskirts of a city.

13.1   *A precious survival needing reinstatement—Marino*

Post-war Development

Partially as a result of state-imposed restrictions in the use of materials and the post-war channeling of scarce investment, but primarily as a consequence of the rise in dwelling standards and the need to supply an insatiable demand for housing, estates planned in the 'fifties and 'sixties almost invariably lacked new local services. There were no pubs, corner shops, community halls or other social, religious or commercial facilities. Consequently, religious, commercial, benevolent and state undertakings seeking to supply new communities with churches, schools, dispensaries, bingo halls, banks, post offices and libraries now invariably find the location and assembly of sites extremely difficult in existing or already-planned housing areas.

Not infrequently, central city facilities abandoned by the urban exodus (churches, pubs, cinemas) must first be disposed of at existing use-value before they can be re-provided in suburban areas. In the scramble for scheduled development land, restricted building finance, lucrative chain tenants and prime site location, much is done without either the knowledge of residents or of clear control by the planning authority.

As the city expands outwards, new and existing low density housing layouts place an intolerable burden on services. Car parking and road requirements produce flat, arid suburbs, while radial and cross-city highways threaten to obliterate the city on which these suburbs depend.

Middle Suburbs

Infill may be defined as the conscious or unconscious placing of new buildings or facilities in suburban areas in a manner which is intended to contribute to and improve their quality. Successful infill is generally a matter of the conscious urbanization of that quality. A glance at the map of Dublin shows that the problems of infill are as various and complex as the suburbs are extensive.

The pattern set by 18th century speculative housing continued into the victorian period, and the resulting urban tissue—the calm organic growth of the city, the quiet harmony of brick walling, slate roofs and careful paving—provided a varied pattern of streets and housing set in well-landscaped gardens. Those areas closest to the city (centres such as Rathmines, for example) are now under heaviest pressure from an increased volume of traffic, car parking, services and range of dwelling type.

The problems in these areas are extensive but identifiable, and their solution highlights the problems met elsewhere.

Planning

To provide the necessary framework, facilities which are required today place great responsibility on the local authority. It is essential that city planning organisation be more closely identified with the principal suburban areas. A proper analysis must be made of area requirements to ensure that clear action-planning for suburbs is initiated and properly correlated with the overall city plan; action plans must be ready in good time.

Encouragement of local bodies and representatives must be a continuing policy on the part of the authorities and a local planning office for each area should be set up to give such encouragement and to

13.2   *Mixed-use infill of appropriate scale*

correlate development in a positive rather than a merely negative manner.

Architectural Problems

The architectural problems relating to infill vary depending on the location, the type of street, and the presence or absence of landscape features.

(a)   **Existing Corridor Streets or Roads**
In streets and roads where the buildings are connected, infill should respect the scale, texture, height and character of existing buildings.

Some streets possess such a strong architectural quality that unit infill should be in total reproduction of the existing facade. Such quality is less often found in the outer suburbs; where it exists, it should be respected.

Respect for existing buildings can be re-echoed in new building form relying mainly on use of materials and control of heights to ensure acceptability of new proposals.

(b)   **Open Streets**
Streets or roads with varied building forms and heights can accept new infill provided that awareness of the existing buildings is evident in the new proposals. It is of importance that existing trees and landforms be retained and that additional work be initiated to make new buildings fit in with the existing townscape.

(c)   **Existing Physical Features**
The complete destruction of existing boundary walls, areas and railings on sites in which infill is projected is common—and deplorable. Retention of such features often enriches the new development and help to knit it into the surrounding area.

(d)   **Construction and Materials**
New building will generally differ in construction from the building being replaced. Due to the size of new units, there is often a serious clash in scale when these are placed in existing suburban locations. In the suburbs, brick has proved a very efficient, suitable and economic material for many years. Skilful design of new infill carrying on this brick tradition can ensure a continued harmony, particu-

larly where the designer accepts the problem of contemporary self-expression in this traditional, versatile yet ever-new material. Modern architecture is continually developing and inventiveness in the use of traditional materials in a new manner has often resulted in a very high standard of infill buildings.

(f) Detail

In inner suburban areas there is considerable erosion of the urban fabric which could and should be prevented by present legislation. The destruction of front and rear gardens for use as tarmac car parks is a regularly-recurring phenomenon. Such development is often carried out without planning permission, and it invariably destroys the pleasant relationship between buildings and gardens in many suburban areas. To overcome this, it is evident the authorities must encourage:—

i. more sensitive design and landscaping of such areas.
ii. development of communal garage or parking areas.

13.3   *By-law setbacks can destroy established features*

iii. improvement of municipal transport facilities.
iv. more rational policy regarding parking provisions.

The extension of parking meters should be re-examined with a view to discontinuing these and replacing them with the superior Scandinavian card system.

Streetscape

Dublin possesses a fine heritage of streetscape which unfortunately is being repressed or replaced by articles and materials of inferior design.

(a) Iron Railings and Details

Encouragement should be given to the retention of iron railings. It may be desirable for the local authorities to collect and store unwanted ironwork for re-use on alternative sites.

(b) Textures

Dublin's streets and pathways were traditionally paved in stone or wooden sets and granite slabs. These have long since been removed and replaced by tarmacadam and concrete paving stones. A deliberate policy of

retention of these should be made for areas which particularly depend on their character.

(c) Light Standards

Traditional lamp standards often display great character and a splendid quality of design. Consideration should be given to improving the design quality of new light fittings as also to the possible retention of the existing fittings, altered or supplemented to provide a better source of light.

Open Spaces

Slowly, many of the inner city's vacant lots and open spaces have been built over or lost to road widening.

(a) Irreplaceable institutional open spaces disappear at an alarming rate—Ballsbridge botanic gardens, for example. Immediate special legislation is needed to restrict site coverage.

(b) Mews developments frequently destroy rear gardens, particularly in cases where blanket set-back requirements for unlikely new roads produce unwanted front gardens to the mews. Plot ratio and set-back requirements must be re-examined on a wider basis to produce a better answer than the present one. Traffic must be restricted in these areas and the narrow lanes and high walls retained; where possible, agreement should be reached on sympathetic materials for walls and roofs; this should be made a condition of planning permission.

(c) The victorians used chance and planned open spaces to provide our present city parks. It is quite clear that on present performance open space in new housing areas will never match up to the high standard set by the great city parks of the past such as Herbert or Palmerston. It is important to achieve a continuance of public parks throughout the city fabric. Consequently, the 10% open space requirement in housing area planning should be replaced by the obligation to make extensive, firm and appropriate landscape proposals. Furthermore, for each open space planted in a new area, an equal contribution ought be made to the authorities towards the cost of landscaping existing built-up areas. Alternatively, to achieve continuity, action planning by the local authority must be employed to inject such parks in existing areas or provide for new park-

land in new development. Where landscape features already exist, they should be integrated with new parks proposals; elsewhere, they should be created anew—as was done at Fairview after land reclamation in the 'twenties.

Such provisions could be initiated by eliminating the blanket 10% open-space requirement in housing area planning, replacing it with firm action plans and leaving the developer responsible only for gardens and small paved areas, plus a cash contribution towards the cost of a really comprehensive parks system.

Large Scale Redevelopment

In broad principle, new infill in the middle suburbs is most successful when limited to the existing scale and usage of the area; large-scale re-developments in existing street or road patterns must be governed by inherent site restrictions in regard to the general characteristics of the area, by respect for building heights and lines, and by the sympathetic use of materials.

Traffic

Heavy concentrated traffic and car parking requirements have a particularly devastating effect on existing smaller-scale middle suburbs. This can only be alleviated by complex traffic-flow planning, by a clear system of segregated pedestrian precincts, and a concentrated effort to provide new off-street car parking space.

Outer Suburbs

The outer suburbs may broadly be described as those areas built on the city's perimeter after the foundation of the state. The problem, as suburbs expand outwards, is again a matter of urbanization. The areas concerned far exceed the area of the middle and inner city, and they lend themselves to an infinite range of solutions. The provisions required may in general be considered under two headings:

(a) The creation of a more functional, practical and visually stimulating environment for residents and

(b) The provision of adequate links between separate identifiable suburbs and the city as a whole.

13.4   *Ten percent open space—unenclosed, unmaintained*

13.5   *Open space without maintenance attracts dumping*

Social Aims

Provide a framework for local participation in planning by the creation of a separate development council for each district.

Aim at the breakdown of social stratification which has given rise to the provision of solely public-sector housing in Finglas, Ballyfermot, Ballymun and Coolock and solely private-sector housing in Foxrock, Dundrum, Churchtown and Lucan. It may be that this is best achieved in new areas by elimination of the present methods of housing assistance and the replacement of this with personal aid to home purchase. Such a policy would require longer mortgages (perhaps state-guaranteed) and greater aid to prospective house purchasers; but it might well result in more varied and more useful house forms — such for example as multiple-occupancy units, maisonettes or three-storey town houses with a 'granny flat' at ground level.

Functional Requirements

Aim at the early provision for a range of functional needs in existing and new areas:

   a. Shopping centres, planned in advance for overall demand rather than as a result of speculative guesswork.

   b. Industrial estates planned to provide local labour.

   c. Office areas planned for the same reason.

   d. Local social buildings (possibly forming part of shopping precincts) such as theatres, halls, and swimming pools.

   e. Schools, creches and senior-citizen facilities should be considered for multiple usage.

   f. Parks as described above, as distinct from barren open spaces.

The provision of these items can best be arranged by the creation of firm local action plans and by a clear relationship established between the local authority, private development companies, and the community itself.

Architectural Quality

Earlier housing areas laid considerable emphasis on privacy and low density. Mass-produced individualised housing units were laid out with a consistency of material and design to produce a harmonious entity.

In contrast, the quality of newer housing areas varies considerably, from the tolerable to the very bad. A thorough investigation of existing new housing areas is urgently needed to identify their individual characteristics before reasonable standards of design can be reimposed. It is essential that design limiting factors laid down by the local authority should take account of these characteristics and firmly incorporate them in projected housing areas.

Community groups can organize:—

   a. To remove disused television masts.

   b. To control and harmonise — but certainly to allow — personal additions such as garden walls, railings, mock facings and aggressive colouring (an extension of the Tidy Towns idea to metropolitan communities).

   c. To control and encourage the replacement of ill-proportioned window frames and other opes.

   d. To control and replace location signs with good lettering.

   e. To ensure that articles and services provided by statutory bodies are of high design standard and in

13.6   *Seemliness, order and discipline*

13.7   *Good marriage of old and newer building*

13.8   *Importance of retaining trees and boundaries*

13.9   *The same lesson as 13.8*

13.10   *Nature and architecture as foil to each other*

conformity with the character of the area.

f. To seek the assistance of local bodies and professional institutes to organize area schedules for painting and decorating and to arrange instalment plans or reduced rates with paint suppliers and decorating firms; and

g. To plan the principles of step-by-step maintenance and upgrading of the area as a whole.

Zoning

It is necessary to re-examine and supplement zoning regulations in order to scale down scheduled areas and fill them out in far greater detail so as to allow greater variety of use. This would generate colour and interest in scale and occupancy.

Estate Layout

Insistence on fixed numbers of houses per acre and regulated garden depths in entire areas, together with blanket regulations covering road-widths, have resulted in complete districts of arid housing layout. Without departing from the merits of existing legislation, what is needed is a wider vocabulary of planning forms and a more detailed, selective and localised application of subsidiary regulations which would result in a more varied system of road grading and a more interesting and wider variety of house types.

It is essential:—

a. To supplement existing regulations which now require the same blanket width for a small cul de sac as for an open highway. A hierarchy of road functions must be determined in advance and adhered to.

b. That regulations be altered to permit public services to be laid not only in roadways, as they now are, but preferably in pedestrian pathways and scheduled open spaces. The possibility of common service ducting underground must be carefully re-examined.

c. To diversify regulations on minimum garden depths to allow these to be applied according to the real requirement of individual sites rather than to a rigid standard. New regulations might best be modelled on the use of daylight protractors rather than relying on arithmetical 'rule of thumb'.

d. To create a realistic policy for open space, not 'space left over after planning'.

Each of the new outer suburbs may be taken as a case in support of these general recommendations for the rationalisation of housing regulations and the de-centralisation subsidiary planning control. Finglas, with a population of 50,000 and an area larger than some of the country's principal cities, as a particular case in point. The predominant one-class, social structure, the bleak housing estates, the poor standards of design and the absence of community facilities are the product of departmentalised and unbalanced planning control. Lack of both planned incentives or clear directions to development agencies result in the belated provision of community services (offices, shops, libraries, police stations, swimming pools and post offices) long after the housing itself has been planned, laid out and even constructed and occupied.

The problem now presented to the new residents of Finglas (as elsewhere, even in developments as yet not begun) is quite needlessly one of 'suburban infill'. These new and growing communities deserve better than the planners and the professions have been able or willing to give them.

13.11   Typical post-war ribbon infill

13.12   What the by-laws do to the street

13.13   High-rise building has not proved the answer

13.14   The "heart" of Finglas, still waiting to beat

13.15   Social facilities bisected by main road—Finglas

13.16   Suburban ribbon housing with unplanned through access

13.17   Road improvements transfer traffic jams, not remove them

13.19   Trees help here—but not much

13.18   Trees need maintenance as well as preservation

13.20   Seemliness is possible

13.21 Pembroke Road—original site

13.22 Pembroke Road—the completed building

Case Study 2 — Inner Suburbs

Project Pembroke Road: Reconstruction to office usage of five georgian houses

General
This study demonstrates the problems of physical infill in a strongly articulated street pattern. The five houses constituted part of a strong phalanx of georgian houses in the inner middle suburbs.

The houses, built about 150 years ago, were in a dilapidated condition and suffered serious structural as well as usage faults.

The Corporation zoned the area in 1964 Draft Plan Residential and Office usage with a site development of 2:1.

Area of site	=	20,000
Development	=	40,000

Notes
Outline planning permission was obtained in 1964 on a proposal to develop:
   a. Hotel facility.
   b. Office Development.

In 1968 full planning permission was obtained for the present built development.

The scheme as built was projected to fit into the georgian street. As no complete reconstruction was demanded by the corporation the architects endeavoured to design a building that would fit into the existing environment.

Results
The building was designed in two blocks:
   1. Low block of three storeys on Pembroke road, in sympathy with georgian facades but not copying them.

   2. Five storey building over basement car park, profiled and well set back to avoid the effect of being too evident from Pembroke road.

Structure
Reinforced concrete but brick-wrapped to sympathise with the existing environment. The brick facade on Pembroke road was designed in detail as a skin subtly reflecting the reinforced concrete framework rather than implying any compressive load bearing structural quality.

Streetscape
Entrances were placed at high level to associate with the similar principle of replaced and adjoining houses.

Criticism
1. The intentions of the architect were overburdened by the 2:1 plot ratio, which resulted in:

   a. Excessively high development of the rear building.
   b. The reduced usage of adjoining garden areas.

Obviously such a ratio development was too high for the site.

2. The architects accepted the insoluble problem of designing to fit into the strong georgian framework. The results although not entirely unsuccessful on the Pembroke road elevation must strengthen the case for:
   a. Completion of new buildings to match identically the adjoining houses.
   b. Where the authority does not impose such regulations the extreme alternative of complete area redevelopment should be examined.

3. **Materials.** The architects attempted seriously to build with a brick that would fit in, accepting a dull brown colour for this reason. Brick weathers and it is important to remember, in selecting it, preferably to select a brick (allowing for weathering) too bright than one that "easily" fits in.

4. **Detail.** Repeat of slate finish to penthouse instead of glass would have been more functional as well as providing a further link to existing slate roofs. It would be preferable if such projections were reduced or eliminated.

5. **Usage.** The usage of the existing buildings was primarily residential; although outside the hands of the architect, clear zoning by the Corporation would have preserved this site for some housing. Residential/offices use — is obviously making the site a commercial development only. The Corporation should therefore define precisely such terms to avoid future reduction of the residential areas.

6. **Conclusions.** Future infill policy must consider carefully:—
   Colour: Note long term requirements.
   Height: To be considered from all aspects.
   Scale: Ditto.
   Texture: Ditto.
   Detail: To interpret or copy.
   Usage: Clearer definitions by planning authority.
   Plot Ratio: To be considered on a wider basis than presently judged.

Editor's Note: This is one of a number of case studies prepared by Patrick Rooney which had to be withheld for lack of space.

A Building Height Strategy for Dublin

by Brian Hogan

Assuming a given site of 2000 m², and a maximum permissible plot ratio of 2.5 to 1 (giving a development potential of 5000 m² of gross floor area), the following six examples show how the feasibility of achieving the plot ratio, the form of the building, and the site planning, are affected by varying limits to building height. In examples (a) to (e), it is assumed that the distance between the buildings and the party boundaries should not be less than half the building height.

The examples show that a high plot ratio combined with severe height restriction produces bad site planning and unsatisfactory open spaces at ground level. Building form is dictated solely by the ad-hoc geometry of planning constraints, regardless of architectural criteria.

a. Deep-space air-conditioned building
 Maximum permissible height: 3 floors (10 m)
 Set-back of 5 m from three party boundaries
 Area per floor 1400 m². Gross area 4200 m².
 Maximum possible plot ratio: 2.1 to 1

b. Naturally-ventilated "narrow" buildings
 Maximum permissible height 3 floors (10 m)
 Set-back from party boundaries 5 m, except on frontage (terrace) block
 Area per floor 1222 m². Gross area 3666 m².
 Maximum possible plot ratio: 1.8 to 1

c. Deep-space air-conditioned buildings
 Maximum permissible height 5 floors (16.5 m)
 Set-back from party boundaries 8.25 m.
 Area per floor 1047 m². Total floor area 5235 m².
 Maximum possible plot ratio: 2.6 to 1

d. Naturally-ventilated "narrow" building
 Maximum permissible height 5 floors (16.5 m)
 Set-back from party boundaries 8.25 m, except on frontage block
 Area per floor 1066 m². Total floor area 5330 m².
 Maximum possible plot ratio: 2.65 to 1

e. Medium-width air-conditioned buildings
 Maximum permissible height 8 floors (26.5 m)
 Set-back from party boundaries 13.25 m.
 Area per floor 596 m². Total floor area 4770 m².
 Maximum possible plot ratio: 2.35 to 1

f. Tower block, air-conditioned
 Maximum permissible height 15 floors (50 m)
 Minimum set-back from party boundaries 13.25 adequate under any circumstances)
 Area per floor 342 m². Total floor area 5178 m².
 Possible plot ratio: 2.55 to 1
 (This solution would only be economical on a much larger site)

Introduction

The purpose of this Study is to examine the question of building height as an element in the urban landscape, and to suggest an approach whereby the height of new buildings can be proposed in a creative rather than repressive way for the enhancement of the view of the city. The evolution of the city's skyline can be directed by design, and good design must have a hard core of logic. This design logic can only be established by an analysis of all the existing factors which seem to be relevant to the problem: nevertheless the *rationale* will inevitably be subjective, depending on the relative weight given by the designer to the various criteria which he has identified. The success or otherwise of a policy in the environmental field ultimately depends on the "reasonableness" with which the facts have been interpreted: the balanced view will usually prevail.

The question of building-height in Dublin is an emotional and subjective one at the present time, particularly in relation to "tall" buildings. Yet in certain situations a new building can be too low, or existing streets may be flawed by a few old buildings which, because of the irregularity of their roofline, detract from the consistency of the street as a whole. In other areas (particularly the newer suburbs) the universal two-storey roofline is excessively monotonous: the eye searches in vain for a focus or landmark.

But we will be pressed first of all to define what is a tall building, and there is only one answer; if a building in a given context looks tall, it *is* tall. A four-storey building in a two-storey housing scheme is tall; so is Liberty Hall. The victorian Freemasons' Hall in georgian Molesworth street must have looked (and was surely intended to look) tall when it was new; but we have become accustomed to its bizarre presence. All depends, literally, on the viewpoint: how near you are to the building, how much you can see of it, how it compares with the general building height around it, and its relationship to the landscape. Dublin has been uniquely endowed by tree-planting: a great many of the trees lining or visible from our public roads are the equivalent of four or five stories in height. Indeed, some might argue that providence has magically ordained that the Dublin "tree-line" and the georgian roofline should coincide. The fact remains that, including 7 towers at Ballymun, only 20 new buildings in Dublin are over nine floors in height (say 100 feet). Stated in those terms the problem would not appear to be very serious: yet it is this very scarcity of taller buildings which renders them noticeable and controversial in our low-profile city.

Accepting that the planning authority sets a limit (the "plot ratio") to the amount of floor space that can be constructed on a given site, why do men need to build high when a low building of the same floor area apparently makes much more sense? Quite simply, it is an innate urge which cannot be suppressed, and the reasons always seem good at the time: to open up a maximum amount of site area for landscaping, to take advantage of a view, to make a monument, to create a marketing "gimmick", to utilise to the full an industrialised building system, or just to make a beautiful well-proportioned building. This recurring urge, however irrational, should be acknowledged and, for the benefit of the urban landscape, in certain locations be positively encouraged.

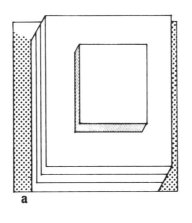

a

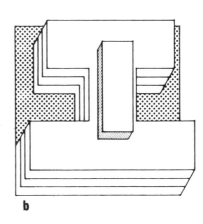

b

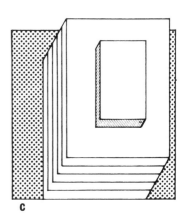

c

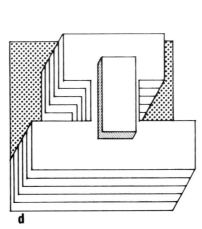

d

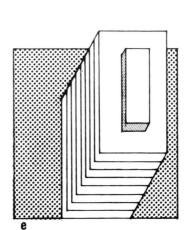

e

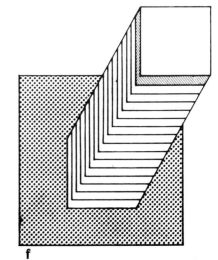

f

The Method

The desirable attributes of a case study of this kind are that it should be based on a simple and practical method, the proposals should be readily understandable, the resultant strategy should be easy to implement, capable of elaboration in detail within the general framework, and flexible enough to permit amendment in the light of experience.

The study method in this instance involves, firstly, the formulation of an architectural attitude to building height in general. Next, the provisions of the Development Plan (1971) in that respect are critically examined. This leads to the identification of some elements in the structure of the city which would appear to be relevant to our consideration of building height in the context of the city as a whole: suburban centres, landmarks and monuments, the city's "edges" (the boundaries between built-up areas and large open spaces), the topographical configuration of the city land, and those areas which are generally agreed to have a high amenity-value. From those overlapping elements a composite picture emerges which will enable a broad strategy to be deduced. The study concludes with some recommendations for further action with a view to developing the strategy to the point where it can become a workable tool in the promotion and guidance of new development.

A View on Building Height

The urge to build high is "irrational". In terms of the convenience of the occupants, the usefulness of the floor space, the capital cost of a building and its cost-in-use, and its impact on the city at ground level, building low is better value in every sense than building high. The taller the building, the more it must rely on mechanical and electrical hardware to enable it to function. It is unnecessary to be a committed doom-watcher to agree that low-energy shelter is a rational objective: it is also consistent with the norms appropriate to a developing country. Something is surely amiss when, as at present, fireplaces are obligatory in low-income housing and total air-conditioning appears to be equally obligatory in "prestige" office buildings. It should be said, however, that the recent dramatic increase in the cost of primary fuels, and the growing sophistication of building users, are rapidly eroding the latter philosophy. While it can be argued that sealed and air-conditioned buildings are the only solution to providing acceptable accommodation in urban sites with frontages on major traffic routes, the fact remains that traffic-noise problems can often be solved by astute site planning and by manipulating the internal layout of the building so that noisy functions (typing pools, punch-card operating, canteens etc.) are located close to the traffic frontage.

Whatever about traffic noise, the real pressure to build taller and/or technically sophisticated buildings derives from the plot ratio provisions of the Dublin Development Plan. The central area inside the canals is allocated a maximum plot ratio of 2.5 to 1 for General Business and 2 to 1 for Residential and Offices: in suburban areas, Residential Services zoning can also have a plot ratio of 2 to 1. The cost of any site is based primarily on the assumption that the maximum plot ratio can be realised in development; and it is the architect's first task to demonstrate that he can deliver the goods in terms of floor area. With the present height restrictions and plot ratio levels, the architect has three choices: to respect the frontage line and height and go

a bit higher at the back, hoping to avoid rights-of-light problems and overlooking, often producing unsatisfactory spaces at ground level, and knowing that if the same solution were adopted on adjoining sites soulless lightwells would be reproduced *ad infinitum*. Alternatively, he can grasp the nettle and propose a significantly taller and more expensive building set back from the street with space around it, thereby committing his client to a time-consuming battle with the local authority, the civic groups and the Minister. The architect must again know that if the same policy were followed next door (and why not? every planning decision can be a "precedent") the scale and texture of the city will be radically altered.

His third option, if he cannot achieve a satisfactory site plan based on natural ventilation (restricted block widths) he can usually succeed by persuading his client to adopt air-conditioning. The significance of the air-conditioned building is that it can have a "deep" plan shape, simplifying the overall geometry and providing maximum floor space within a given area of perimeter wall. The building will of course be significantly more expensive to build and to operate than it might have been. 14.0 attempts to illustrate the relationship between building height and plot ratio, by taking as an example an "average" theoretical site of 2,000 square metres with one street frontage and a plot ratio of 2.5 to 1. Varying height constraints are applied and the recurring problems identified.

It is difficult to avoid the conclusion that, firstly, plot ratios should be reduced in areas of height restriction, and secondly that the growing conflict between the ever-increasing comfort expectations of building users and conversely the need to limit energy consumption, has produced new problems in terms of building science which architects and consulting engineers are ill-equipped to deal with. In the teaching of building construction and design, are the blind still leading the blind?

It might be argued that I have over simplified the complex relationships between the shape of a site, planning controls, and building form; my object primarily has been to emphasise these relationships in the context of building height, because experience suggests that the city planners have not realised their

importance. It might also be argued that if and when cheap energy eventually flows from the Celtic Sea, new conditions conducive to tall buildings will prevail. Maybe so: but the deliberate waste of fuel, whether it be cheap or dear, is difficult to justify. And what can be done about the idealist, the egoist, or the inspired entrepreneur who still, in spite of all, can only find fulfilment in designing or owning the tallest building in town? Nothing: except to point to the map and say "you can't do it here: but if you must, why not try it out *there*?"

The Present Policy

The Dublin Development Plan (1971) incorporates objectives in relation to building height and high buildings. (The references are set out in Appendix A). A high building is defined by the planning authority as "a building significantly higher than neighbouring or surrounding development." Map 2 of the Plan shows those areas in which "high buildings will be prohibited". The prohibited area is comparatively small in extent, and the Written Statement goes on to say that in all other areas of the city, "high buildings may be permitted but each application will be considered on its merits". There follows a list of criteria which would be applied in considering any proposal for a high building. They include:

The proper planning of the area.
Intrusion on existing development patterns, sky-lines, architectural groups or landscapes.
The visual significance of the location.
The size of the site.
Overshadowing and the effect on neighbours' development possibilities.
Contribution to the general character of the area and relationship to other high buildings.
Relationship to open spaces and the Liffey.
Vehicular access facilities.
Traffic capacity of adjoining streets.

14.2 *Shaded area shows how creative building height policy could reinforce visually the effect of higher ground at the town centre*

While the phrase "in all other areas" may sound unduly permissive, the above-listed criteria, if rigorously applied, could constitute a fairly effective embargo on all high buildings, whatever their proposed location. It is argued by the planning authority (page 1 of the Development Plan) that the aim is to "formulate general policies", and that as time passes particular aspects "will be subject to detailed design where problems are urgent or development pressures are expected . . . .". It could be argued conversely that the objectives on building height are too vague, and that they have been shown to be ineffective in a number of cases. The problem is certainly urgent and worthy of detailed study. Indeed the planning authority is in a uniquely fortunate position compared with its counterparts in other capitals (London, Paris, Brussels) in that the scarcity of high buildings in Dublin provides the opportunity for a creative approach; but this demands skilled manpower, time and commitment. The absence of these three inputs were glaringly noticeable in the Central Bank fiasco: a classic case in which all the parties concerned were the losers.

How effective is the present height policy? Within the limited area in which tall buildings are prohibited, at least five have been built in recent years. Furthermore, the boundary of the "prohibited" zone is tightly drawn around areas of high environmental amenity with the result that a number of new high buildings are threatening the amenity of those areas which the height zoning seeks to protect. Again, while the residential areas south of the Grand canal are included in the objective which states that "development of any kind which affects the continuity of the present . . . rooflines will not be permitted" and lays down a height limit of 60 feet, those areas are not included in the hatched portions of the Map indicating height restriction. While the stated objective is to prohibit high buildings "in close proximity to important landmarks", those landmarks are not scheduled: the question is begged — *what* landmarks, and *how* close?" Finally, while the Plan in effect says that high buildings may be acceptable anywhere outside the area of height restriction, it does not identify locations in which taller structures might be positively encouraged.

The present policy, therefore, seems to lack commitment and precision; as a result, it has not induced a consensus view; and it will therefore be under continuous assault from those who believe that in their development, wherever it might be, a tall structure is the answer. In the absence of consensus, the battle is fought *ab initio* in each case, to the exhaustion and frustration of the promoter, his architect, and the hard-pressed officials of the planning authority; and doubtless to the irritation of the confused citizen.

Map 14.1 shows the area of building restriction defined in the Development Plan (1971) and the location of buildings completed in the recent past which are significantly higher than the established building height in their vicinity.

Landmarks and Monuments

The city is in one sense an aggregation of standard self-effacing structures of different periods punctuated by larger individual buildings of positive character. These old public buildings have developed a hereditary *persona* and they fulfill a number of useful functions in the urban landscape. They develop a kind of gravitational field so that they tend to constitute the centre of an area or precinct: they are oases of variety and interest which enliven the many parts of the city which even Dublin's best friends would admit were dull; and finally, they provide a network of landmarks, or "mute signals", which guide us through the city. It is quite normal to help the enquiring pedestrian on his way with an instruction like this:

"Look it's quite simple: down past the Pillar it's gone now, straight up past Findlater's church with the big spire bear right at the top past another church and the Mater on your right then left at the traffic lights to Doyle's corner Doyle is gone this long time straight on bearing left at Phibsboro' church dead ahead past a big new brown gazebo and the cattle market it's closed down of course carry right on through the white gates and the Hollow is down on your left you can't miss it."

There are three points to note from that oration. Firstly, the route was described in terms of landmarks which are generally buildings: secondly, some of the landmarks *no longer exist* except in the folk memory of the people. Doyle's corner will never become Murphys; and the "cattle market", when developed (as is intended) as a paradise of urban living by Dublin Corporation, will still conjure up the lowing of the beasts, the silver-painted stalls, and above all that interesting smell that assailed us in our youth as we rattled down the North circular road on top of the number 9 tram. As for the Pillar, although gone some eight years, the only possible explanation for its continued use as a landmark is that a large number of citizens, when gazing down O'Connell street, still actually see it. And finally, a high proportion of the landmarks are church spires, which still pierce the Dublin skyline in almost islamic profusion.

Old landmarks, therefore, must be valued and respected. Map 14.2 identifies a selection of the more generally known Dublin landmark buildings and monuments; it does not pretend to be exhaustive. While many of the items may also appear in the preservation schedules in the Development Plan, others do not. For example, the great gasometer on the south quays and the flour mill on Grand canal basin are two magnificent 20th century landmarks; the former effectively ruins the great Fitzwilliam street vista (a classic case of bad siting) and the second does no harm at all. It is clear that a statutory listing of landmarks *per se* is urgently required for inclusion in the revised City Plan in 1976, with appropriate policies relating to preservation, retention or replacement.

The map also identifies particular landmarks which, because of their architectural and monumental qualities, would be particularly affected by new taller structures in their vicinity. The implications of a zone of height restriction within a radius of 200 metres of each "sensitive" landmark is also shown by a circle drawn to scale.

Not all "monuments" are landmarks: indeed Dublin is under-equipped with structures which serve no useful purpose, but which have a purely symbolic or decorative function: only a very few significant works of public sculpture have been given to the city since the nineteenth century and many older ones have been destroyed. Therefore our few major monuments need space to "breathe", and while this is best provided by a creative approach to surrounding pedestrian surfaces and traffic circulation, some are large enough to constitute landmarks and suggest the discouragement of tall new structures in their vicinity.

Local Centres

Map 14.3 locates those older suburban centres or "nodes" which, until fairly recently in Dublin's history, were separate and self-contained places with their own identity. Within the living memory of some of our contemporaries, the journey to Tallaght or even Rathfarnham lay through open fields, and not much earlier there was countryside between the Grand canal and Donnybrook. The destination was clearly in view: a church spire or some other large building marked the centre of the village from afar. In the meantime, two-storey housing has filled in the spaces between these little centres so that their visual identity has been lost. The Development Plan recognises the lack of balance in terms of land use and facilities between the city centre and the middle suburbs (p. 21: Urban Structure) and states that "variations will be used to achieve a desirable form of development which is visually interesting and more efficient. Higher use density will be achieved around district centres . . . ." This aim has not been sufficiently supported by positive measures to encourage its achievement.

To support this point, zones which normally induce "higher use density" are shown in tone on Map 14.3; these are General Business, Residential and Office, Residential Services and (in the case of Dun Laoghaire) Primarily Commercial. It is clear that a more creative approach to zoning and plot ratio is needed in the suburban centres if the objectives of the Development Plans are to be attained.

There is a strong case for encouraging the provision of clusters of significantly-higher residential and commercial units in the suburban centres to re-establish their visual identity vis-a-vis the intervening low-profile infill. Such buildings should not be less than three times the height of the established rooflines: this suggests a minimum height of 90 to 100 feet, assuming that all other considerations such as space around the buildings, ground level amenity, and the degree of overshadowing have been satisfactorily taken into account. The object should be to avoid a diffuse effect: clusters should be recognisable as such (perhaps a minimum of three and a maximum of seven separate units) and the "high building zone" would have to be fairly tightly drawn around each centre: possibly a circle of not more than a quarter of a mile in diameter. The map shows the scale of such circles in relation to each subcentre.

A strategy of this kind would help to implement the planning authority's aims in intensifying the vitality and facilities in the older suburban nodes, and would introduce into the city's skyline a dynamic and stimulating element which is now sadly lacking.

If tall buildings in those centres should have a *minimum* height in relation to the established skyline (half measures would not achieve the visual objectives) should a *maximum* height be laid down? The reality is that if the maximum plot-ratio provisions are observed, the height of a building would be related in practice to the size of the site which it is expedient to assemble; which in turn depends on the norms of market demand. The latter, for the foreseeable future, are likely to involve fairly modest developments rarely exceeding 100,000 square feet in floor area. Under those circumstances the likelihood of a building in excess of twelve to fifteen floors would be remote; indeed, the planners' problem would not be to restrain but to encourage tall buildings where they are needed, in the face of their economic and operational defects.

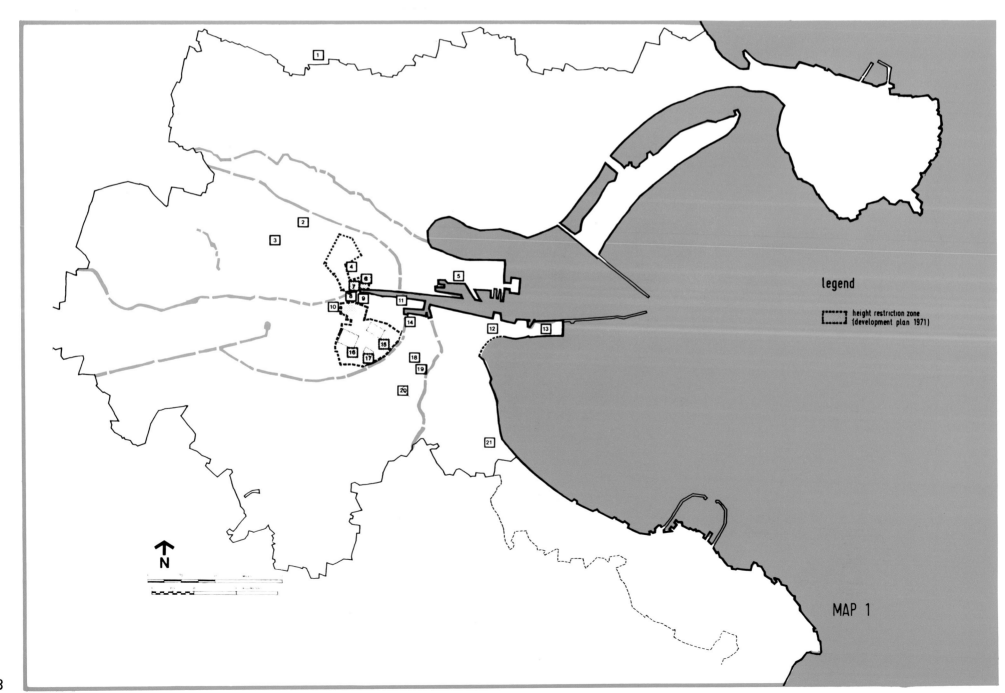

MAP 1: TALL BUILDINGS

Legend

1. Ballymun Towers
2. Phibsboro Centre
3. Park House
4. Office Buildings, Marlborough Street
5. Granary
6. Bus Arus
7. Liberty Hall
8. O'Connell Bridge House
9. Hawkins House
10. Central Bank
11. Gasometer
12. ESB Generating Station
13. ESB Generating Station
14. Boland's Mill
15. Bank of Ireland
16. Sugar Company
17. Fitzwilton House
18. Lansdowne House
19. Hume House
20. Ardoyne House
21. Saint Vincent's Hospital

legend

- - - - height restriction zone
(development plan 1971)

N

MAP 1

MAP 2: MONUMENTS AND LANDMARKS

Legend

1. Bailey Lighthouse
2. Ballymun Towers
3. Finglas Office Building
4. Raheny Church
5. Collins Avenue Church
6. Parnell Round Tower
7. Chapelizod Monument
8. Wellington Monument
9. N.C.R. Office Building
10. Phibsboro Church
11. Phibsboro Office Building
12. Croke Park
13. Mater Hospital
14. Findlaters Church
15. Parnell Monument
16. G.P.O.
17. Four Courts
18. Halfpenny Bridge
19. Liberty Hall
20. Custom House
21. Bus Arus
22. Connolly Station
23. Granary

24. Bull Wall Statue
25. Poolbeg Lighthouse
26. Generating Station
27. Generating Station
28. Ringsend Church
29. Grey Gasometer
30. Hawkins/Tara Street Complex
31. Trinity College Frontage
32. O'Connell Bridge House
33. Bank of Ireland
34. Central Bank
35. Dublin Castle
36. Christchurch Cathedral
37. Heuston Station
38. Royal Hospital
39. Kilmainham Gaol
40. St. Patrick's Cathedral
41. Leinster House
42. Boland's Flour Mill
43. Red Gasometers
44. St. Stephen's Church
45. Bank of Ireland Head Office
46. Sugar Company

47. University College
48. Harcourt St. Office Building
49. Fitzwilton House
50. Haddington Rd. Church
51. Lansdowne Rd. Grandstands
52. Ballsbridge Complex
53. Ardoyne House
54. Burlington Hotel
55. Carroll's Office Building
56. Rathmines Church
57. Rathmines Town Hall
58. Rathgar Church
59. Donnybrook Church
60. Sandymount Tower
61. St. Vincent's Residential Tower
62. R.T.E. Mast
63. Merrion Rd. Building
64. Belfield Water Tower
65. Blackrock Church
66. Monkstown Churches (2)
67. Dun Laoghaire Church Spire
68. Dun Laoghaire Pier
69. Joyce's Tower
70. Dalkey Hill/Killiney Hill

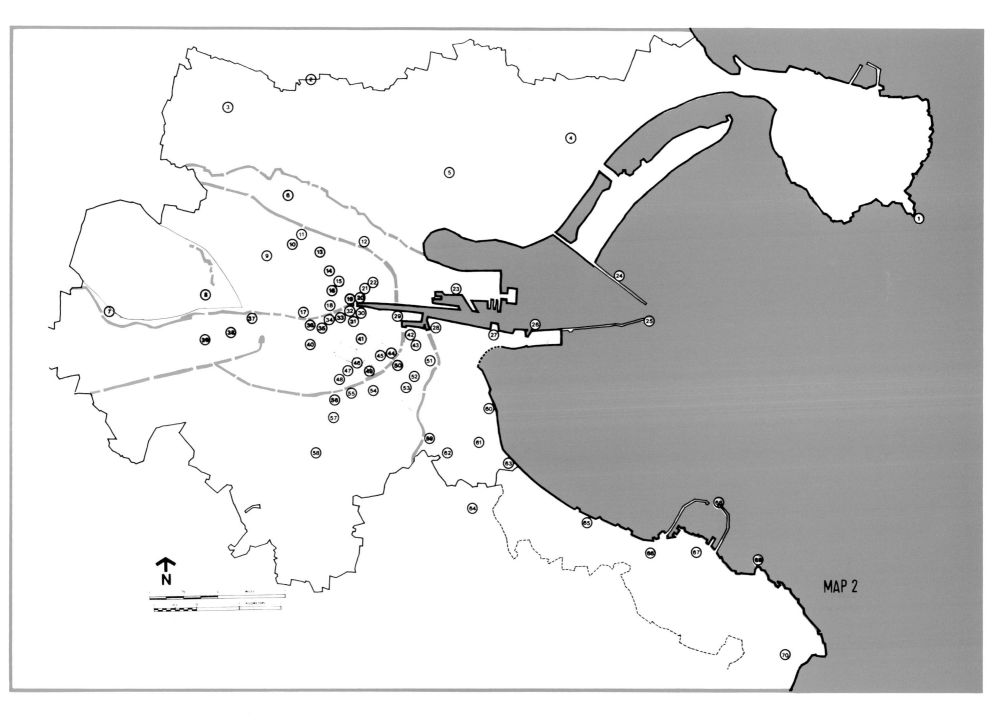

MAP 2

Contours

In general the profile of the city land consists of a gentle rise from the seashore to the higher northern ground and the southern hills, with noticeable but restrained valleys containing the Liffey, the Dodder and the Tolka. The eye looks in vain for dramatic outcrops. Nevertheless, in some isolated instances the contours are compressed and a tangible rise or fall occurs in the urban landscape. Map 14.4 reproduces the contours defined by the Ordnance Survey: unfortunately they are generally at 100 foot intervals which is insufficient to identify adequately some of the smaller variations in ground level which nevertheless can be very noticeable to the pedestrian.

The relevance to this study of such local variations in level derives from the possibility of emphasising and indeed exaggerating the land profile by manipulating the skyline through the medium of building height. This is best illustrated by the example of the view of Dun Laoghaire from the pierheads (14.6). As the land slopes up from the sea a deliberate gradation in the height of new buildings towards the centre of the

town would intensify the effect of a town on a hill. This would conversely involve height restriction on the edges of the town. Similar possibilities exist in the centre of Dublin. The rising ground in the vicinity of Christchurch cathedral (the ancient core of the city) and the slope up to Mountjoy square and Dorset street provide opportunities for the creative design of the profile of the city. The means, however, are not those which have already been proposed for the suburban centres: on the contrary, gradual and localised increase in building height in relation to the established norms is required to make the restrained visual point, which need not necessarily conflict with objectives related to amenity or conservation.

Edges

The urban area either fades away with diminishing density into the surrounding countryside or terminates suddenly at natural or manmade boundaries: those boundaries or edges, in the case of Dublin, are defined by the seashore, the banks of the Liffey, and the larger green spaces within the city itself. In most instances the contact between the tightly-knit weave of buildings

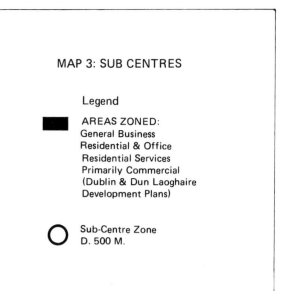

MAP 3: SUB CENTRES

Legend

AREAS ZONED:
General Business
Residential & Office
Residential Services
Primarily Commercial
(Dublin & Dun Laoghaire
Development Plans)

○ Sub-Centre Zone
D. 500 M.

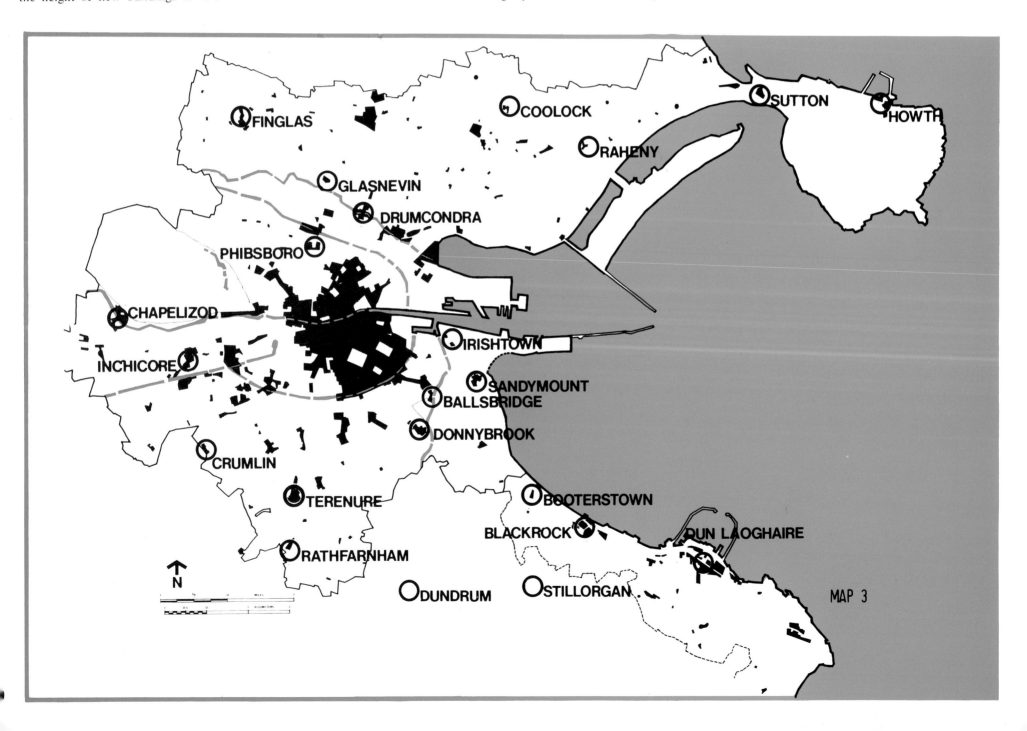

and streets on the one hand, and the open space of the Bay or tree belts of Phoenix park on the other, is sufficiently precise to require no additional emphasis. In certain places, however, there is visually a lack of definition, and the dynamic possibilities of the inherent contrast have not yet been realised in the urban landscape. Trees can be used to great effect in intensifying the degree of edge definition; but that is a long-term process. The inevitable urban motorways will create new and unwanted edges, and great skill in landscaping is required to ensure that their impact on adjoining small-scale residential enclaves is minimised.

Once again, however, where an improvement in the degree of scenic contrast at the edges of the city is required, the most effective means consists of the creative direction and control of building height. Map 4.4 proposes some specific locations in the city where this technique could be applied with advantage.

Orientation is important: a north-facing edge of buildings, seen from afar, might read only as a dark and forbidding wall. On the other hand, south-facing buildings, if visible from a distance, should have light or reflective surfaces to maximise their impact. These considerations are particularly important in relation to the shoreline of the bay. In the case of the Liffey, the great width of the space between the two quayside frontages (likely to be increased with future road-widening) suggests the possibility of a somewhat higher average building height on the quays, and the introduction of short sequences of taller buildings on alternating sides of the river, allowing the numerous bridges to define the "module" of variation on each bank. While the norm would be a continuous frontage a little higher than at present, the modules of taller buildings would be set back from the quay frontages and consist of clearly defined and separate structures. This variety in the form and height of the Liffeyside enclosures should not, however, be such as to affect the unique impact of the broad gently-curving stream and its graceful crossings. Frontage buildings, therefore, should perhaps be restricted to 60 feet in height, and the taller free-standing structures should not exceed 120 feet.

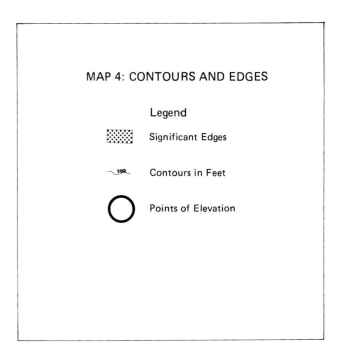

MAP 4: CONTOURS AND EDGES

Legend

Significant Edges

Contours in Feet

Points of Elevation

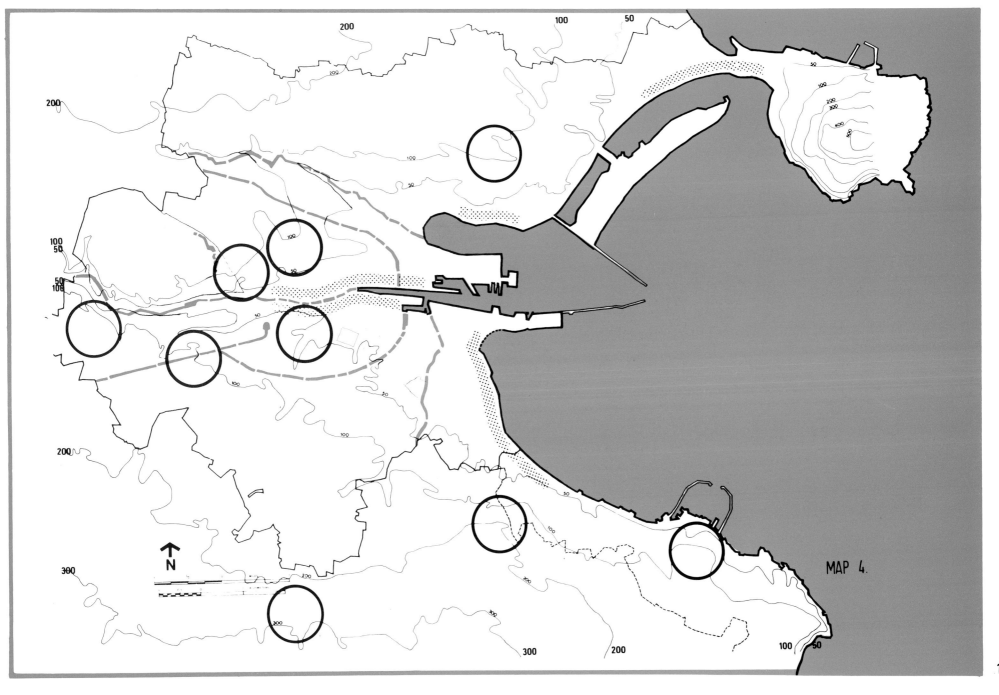

MAP 4.

Dublin Standard Height

Having examined a number of special characteristics or situations in the Dublin urban landscape which seem to constitute the raw materials for the evolution of a new building height strategy, the question is begged: "What about the *non-special* areas in between which constitute the bulk of the city land?" On the one hand rigid height controls would be inappropriate: on the other hand some restraint is necessary if the defined highpoints are to register in the overall profile of the city. We must therefore attempt to define "Dublin standard height".

The areas concerned are predominantly residential in use, traditionally in the form of one to three storey detached, semi-detached or terrace dwellings. The increased pressure on living space with the growth of the city, disenchantment with commuting, greater affluence among the unmarried young and retired couples, is likely to accelerate the demand for apartment living, particularly in the private sector. While a radical overhaul of the whole housing finance system

is needed if a significant increase in privately-built apartments in the central area is to materialise, the trend towards flats and maisonettes is already well established in the inner and middle suburbs. The present residential density provisions of the Development Plan sensibly link density with building height: the permissible number of flats per acre for two storey development is approximately doubled for four floors and over. In the interests of optimum land utilisation in the inner and middle suburbs the maximum utilisation of permissible density should be encouraged; which means the acceptance of four-storey development and over as the norm for apartment buildings. But an upper limit must be defined, thereby establishing Dublin standard height.

We are fortunate in our task. The standard suburban profile has existed for years and is being reinforced as each year passes: *it is, quite simply, the Dublin tree line*. Mature trees in Dublin can grow to a height of 50 to 60 feet. The silhouette of the rising hinterland of the city viewed from Dun Laoghaire pier or the northern

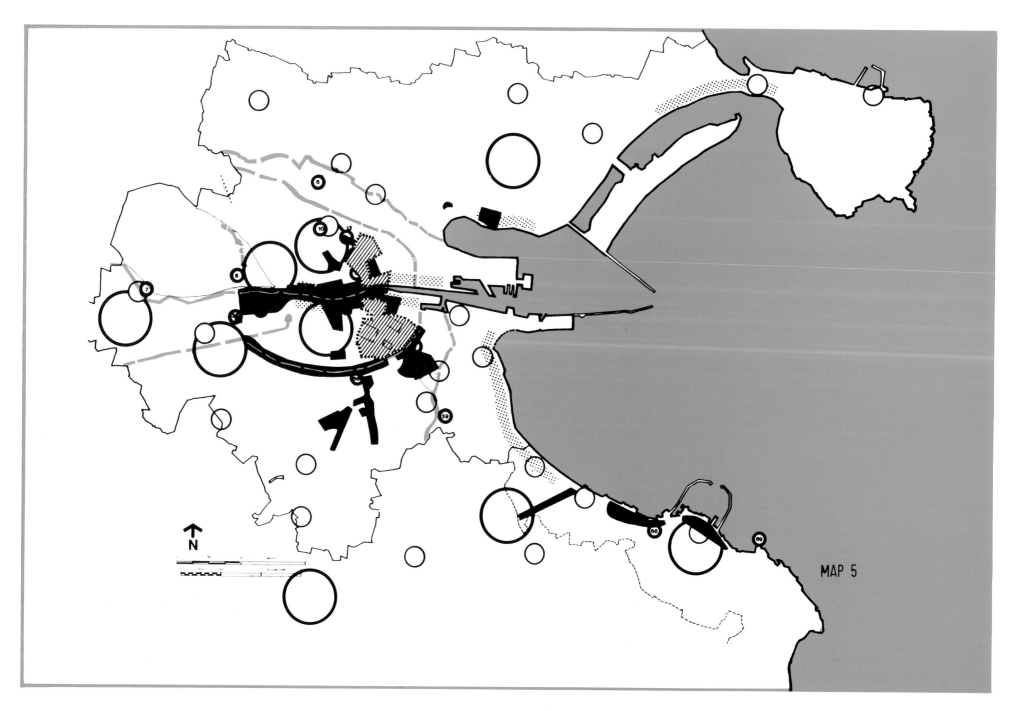

MAP 5: HEIGHT ZONING PROPOSALS

Legend

ZONE 1 — Areas of Height Restriction

— Areas of High Amenity (Development Plan & An Taisce)

— Land within 200 m. of Major Monuments (numbers refer to Map 1)

ZONE 2

— Sub-Centre: No Height Restriction

ZONE 3

— Elevated Areas Suitable For Height Manipulation

ZONE 4

— Edges: Increased Building Height

ZONE 5

— Standard Height Limit (60 feet)

MAP 5

corniche is predominantly the soft outline of a hundred thousand trees. In the "standard" areas of the city, therefore, the aim should be to maintain this sylvan profile, and restrict building height to a maximum of 55 feet or the equivalent of five floors, with no lower limit, thereby encouraging within broad tolerances a welcome variety in the suburban roofline.

In practice the normal constraints arising from considerations such as overlooking and overshadowing (relative to the size of the site) will militate against a five storey solution in many cases. On the other hand, if every permission for new development contained building conditions requiring tree preservation and tree planting, the sylvan character of the inner suburbs would be conserved and newer suburbs, in the course of time, would mellow among growing trees in their turn.

Height Zoning

In proposing a new system of building height zones there is the danger, inherent in all categorisations, of undue rigidity on the one hand and unworkable generalisation on the other. What is intended here is to propose a *method* whereby building height problems might be tackled rationally on the basis of an explicit design policy. Implicit in this approach is the assumption that its city-scale broadness would be subsequently refined through a detailed professional study of particular areas.

The various criteria examined earlier and charted on our maps must be overlapped and integrated to produce a unified concept of the city's skyline: a personal interpretation of such an overlap is shown in Map 14.5. Five zones are identified below, setting out the objectives and suggesting methods for their achievement in each case, hopefully establishing the brief for the further study that would be necessary to transform the strategy into workable tactics for the guidance of planners, developers, builders and the general public.

The question of consensus must be faced: clearly a more sophisticated system of consultation between the planners and the planned-for must be evolved within the local government structure: local and vocational groups are more articulate than ever before, and are utilising professional advocacy to considerable effect, often nullifying the substantial input by experienced public officials on detailed planning proposals which may be subsequently modified or abandoned—bad value for the ratepayer! The vision of the planner and the architect, the courage of the property investor, and the prudent husbandry of the citizen, can surely be reconciled to the benefit of all.

Height Zone 1
Classification
Those areas scheduled in the Development Plan (1971) and in the An Taisce Amenity Study as having high environmental qualities worthy of consideration; the planning authority's Area of Height Restriction; the land within 200 metres of the established boundaries of those areas; and land within a radius of 200 metres of listed landmarks or monuments.

Objective
To secure the preservation of established building lines and parapet lines in conservation areas, and to ensure that the skyline is not broken by new development from the pedestrian viewpoint on listed public thoroughfares.

Method
Schedules of thoroughfares and frontages.
Schedules of landmarks and monuments.
Case studies of pedestrian sightlines in scheduled thoroughfares and public spaces to define appropriate building height contours or "ceilings" in their immediate hinterland.

Regulations defining appropriate tolerances or variations in building height on scheduled frontages.
Reduction of maximum permissible plot ratio to 1.5 to 1 wherever a higher plot ratio now applies.

Height Zone 2
Classification
The lands within an approximate radius of 200 metres of the centre of gravity of scheduled village or neighbourhood sub-centres lying outside the canal ring.

Objective
To restore the visual identity of sub-centres by the provision of a limited cluster of significantly taller buildings in each centre.

Method
Urban design survey of each sub-centre to establish appropriate boundary for Zone 2, and to identify desirable locations for tall structures taking into account existing amenities and established "main street" character.

Regulations to control piecemeal redevelopment within the zone.

Regulations concerning the *minimum* height of tall buildings.

Regulations concerning the appropriate *maximum* floor area for individual buildings.

An architectural policy in relation to building form, encouraging towers rather than slabs (a tower being defined as a structure in which the height is not less than twice its greatest width).

Regulations concerning the distance between new tall buildings and older residential developments.
Maximum permissible plot ratio of 2.5 to 1.

Height Zone 3
Classification
Built-up areas lying on rising ground, or on local elevations in the general topography of the city land, which are not already incorporated in either Zone 1 or Zone 2.

Objective
To add variety to the profile of the city by intensifying the effect of existing variations in ground level through the manipulation of building height.

Method
Topographical study of the city to establish significant local variations in level; selection of appropriate areas for zoning.

Urban design study of each area to establish long-range viewpoints of local height contours map to establish gradations of permissible building height from edge of zone to the centre.

Schedule of thoroughfares and/or frontages to which contour map is applicable.

Height Zone 4
Classification
Linear sectors which constitute visible boundaries between built-up areas and significant open spaces.

Objective
To reinforce the natural boundary between the built-up areas and the major open spaces by manipulating building lines and building heights.

Method
Urban design survey to establish edges which "read" in the context of existing long-range viewpoints.

Delineation of zone boundaries in relation to maximum depth of edge strip required to achieve desired build-up. Regulations concerning minimum and maximum height limits.

Regulations concerning continuity of building lines.
Maximum permissible plot ratio of 2.0 to 1.

Height Zone 5
Classification
All areas of the city not covered by Zones 1 to 4 inclusive.

Objective
To conserve the established standard Dublin skyline (the mature tree line) while encouraging maximum utilisation of urban land within acceptable limits.

Method
Regulations concerning the replacement and/or additional planting of trees in all new developments.
Urban design study to evolve new graded relationships between building height, residential density, plot ratio, and site coverage.
Regulations concerning distances between adjoining buildings related to common site boundaries.
Maximum permissible plot ratio of 1.25 to 1.

APPENDIX A
DUBLIN DEVELOPMENT PLAN
1971 — REFERENCES
3.16   Control in Areas of High Civic Value
    (i) Development should conform to existing building lines and building heights . . . .
4.8   In assessing whether the individual proposal is in accordance with the proper planning and development of the area, it is necessary to relate the broad concepts to . . . . more detailed principles . . . . in the Third Schedule of the Act ("High Buildings" are listed as one of the headings).
8.2   The georgian area to the north east of the city centre
    The Fitzwilliam area
    St. Stephen's Green area
    Residential areas south of the Grand Canal
    The following general principles will be enforced . . . . in the above areas:
    Development of any kind which affects the continuity of the present elevations or rooflines will not be permitted.
8.5   Fitzwilliam area (south city georgian areas) . . . . A general height restriction of 60 feet will be imposed.
8.6   St. Stephen's Green
    2. There will be a limitation on the height of new buildings equivalent to the general cornice level of the eighteenth century houses of four stories . . . .
8.7   Residential areas south of the Grand Canal
    A height restriction of 60 feet will generally be enforced . . . .

8.8 High Building Control

A high building is defined as a building significantly higher than neighbouring or surrounding development. The Planning Authority is aware that high buildings are likely to play an appreciable part in the future development of Dublin and that their siting and design is a matter of importance.

8.9 Prohibited Areas

High buildings will be prohibited in areas of historic or architectural interest, areas in close proximity to important landmarks or areas where they would obscure views or disrupt the scale, skyline or quality of valuable urban spaces. These areas are shown on Map 2 of the Development Plan.

8.10 Areas in which High Buildings may be Permitted

In all areas of the city, excluding those in 8.9 above, high buildings may be permitted but each application will be considered on its merits. The points for consideration in assessing whether such buildings should be permitted are:

i) The proper planning and development of the area, including any provisions of the Development Plan.

ii) Whether the building will disrupt the pattern of existing development or obtrude itself on the skyline to the detriment of existing architectural groups and landscape.

iii) Whether its position has any positive visual or civic significance in relation to the town as a whole.

iv) Whether the site is large enough in relation to its surroundings to allow for erection of a suitably designed base of lower buildings or the provision of open space.

v) The degree of overshadowing of the adjoining area and the extent to which the building would detract from the development possibilities of the adjoining area.

vi) Whether the building makes a better contribution to the general character of the area than possible alternatives and whether it relates satisfactorily to any other existing or proposed high building in the vicinity.

vii) The relationship of the proposed building to existing and proposed open spaces and to the River Liffey.

viii) Whether, in view of its prominence, the design and materials proposed for the building are of sufficiently high quality.

ix) The risk of serious injury to civic dignity and amenity which would result from the placing of inappropriate advertising matter on the building.

x) In the case of residential development the density of development in terms of residential units per acre.

xi) The site coverage and plot ratio of a particular property and those of neighbouring development.

xii) The adequacy of facilities for parking and loading and unloading.

xiii) The capacity of the streets in the immediate vicinity to handle the volume of traffic likely to be generated.

xiv) The uses proposed and permissible.

xv) Conformity with acceptable standards in relation to fire hazard and safety generally.

APPENDIX B
SCHEDULE OF AN TAISCE LISTINGS

Type 1   Major Architectural Merit

Henrietta street — King's Inns.
Merrion square to Fitzwilliam squares.
St. Stephen's Green east and south, including Ely place and Hume street.

Type 2   Distinctive Dublin Character (North City)

Mountjoy square area, including Denmark street, Gardiner street, Belvedere place, Parnell square north, north Great George's street.
Beresford place area.
Inns quay, Arran quay and adjoining area.
Blackhall street and place.
Broadstone and King's Inns area.
Portland row.
Clontarf crescent.

South City

The medieval city including High street, Wood quay and the precincts of Christchurch, St. Patrick's cathedral and St. Audeon's.
South Central area including Dame street, College Green, Grafton street, Nassau street, Dawson street, Molesworth street and Kildare street.
St. Stephen's Green area, including the west and north sides, and Harcourt street.
Leeson street, Baggot street, Hatch street, Wilton place.
Pembroke - Ballsbridge, including Pembroke, Waterloo, Wellington, Raglan, Clyde and Elgin roads, and adjoining minor roads.
Harcourt terrace.
Mount Pleasant square area.
Kilmainham (the Kilmainham Gaol and the Royal Hospital).

Type 3   Scenic Quality

Longford terrace and Seapoint.
De Vesci terrace.
Monkstown church area.
Howth.
Clontarf, Dollymount and north shoreline.
O'Connell street area, including Marlborough street, Parnell square, Moore street, Gardiner street to Dorset street and Eccles street.
Constitution hill (King's Inns and the Broadstone station).
The Liffey quays, north side.

Scenic Quality (South City)

The Liffey quays, south side.
Francis street, Thomas street area.
Kingsbridge area.
Grafton street area.
Lr. Leeson street, Morehampton road.
Kenilworth square; Rathgar area.

Belgrave square area, including Castlewood avenue, Church road, Palmerstown road.
The Grand Canal.
Dodder and Camac rivers.

Dun Laoghaire Borough:
Monkstown road area
Dun Laoghaire.
Killiney; Dalkey.
Merrion avenue.

Note:
In this building height study, Dublin is defined rather artificially as the land enclosed by the county borough and Dun Laoghaire borough boundaries. The strategy and zoning classifications proposed could clearly be extended in principle to apply to all new development areas lying outside those boundaries but still within the built-up areas of the city region.

14.3 The "classic" landmark—St. George's steeple

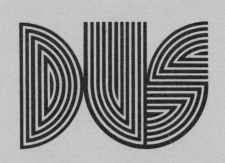

Summary and Conclusions

President and Council, Royal Institute of the Architects of Ireland

1. Dublin Bay and coast amenity must be protected

The shoreline and the bay, part natural and part man-made, is a special and precious asset. It must be conserved and protected. First priorities here include the preservation and improvement of public access for recreation; the control of unsuitable, intrusive or incongruous development, particularly by industry; a total re-appraisal of the proposed coastal motorway; and the proper control and integration of port and harbour development with the city's traffic network and the overall planning and design of the bay as a whole.

2. Rehabilitation of the Liffey and quays must be undertaken

The river Liffey is another unique asset. It forms one of Dublin's great urban spaces, all the more important from its central location and historical associations. Along much of its length, existing buildings are unworthy of their great location. The latter offers unique opportunities for occasional large civic structures sited within a generally smaller framework.

The major obstacle to a fruitful use of this great asset is the problem of pollution of the river waters, with consequent smell nuisance at low tide, especially in hot weather. Many proposals have been put forward for ponding the waters of the river between the tide-line at Kingsbridge and the Custom House, the latest being a study published in September 1975 by the Institute of Research and Standards. The problems here are formidable, since there is not only considerable pollution of the Liffey bed from direct discharge of untreated sewage, but also the even more serious threat of polluted discharge from the Camac river. Any proposal for ponding must be accompanied by provisions for intercepting the flow from this stream and piping it seawards beyond the central city area. The cost of such a project would be considerable; but the benefits as regards the rejuvenation of a major civic asset are incalculable to the city as a whole and to the re-vitalisation of the quays and the local authority should press ahead to determine its flexibility and cost. The recent decision not to incorporate such a barrage in the new river-crossing at Memorial road does not dispose of the matter. An independent barrage could, and should, still be constructed elsewhere as soon as possible.

3. The canals and basins must be preserved primarily as amenity parkways

The Grand canal, thanks to the enlightened decision to lay the main city trunk sewer beside rather than underneath the waterway, serves the south city as an invaluable and unique linear parkway.

The Royal, although now closed to navigation, performs a similar function for the north city; an equally enlightened and courageous decision is now needed to retain it also as recreational and amenity open space, and to re-route the current urban motorway proposal. The present one would destroy this asset for ever. The northern canal has been more neglected of late than the southern, but both need to be upgraded, with preservation and good management of existing trees and the planting of new ones of suitable large species.

Responsibility for the canals, at least within the urban area, should be transferred either to the local authority or the Office of Public Works, and imaginative redevelopment should be planned at nodal points, especially at the harbours and basins of the system.

4. Positive policy, not negative control, is needed to deal with design of infill in existing streets, going beyond mere questions of style, and combining together use and density, site cover, retention or creation of urban space, and policy on bulk and height

The existing fabric of the city, with its strongly established corridor-street patterns, gives rise to special problems of physical and visual disruption. In particular, the large scale of many modern buildings and the need for correspondingly large spaces around and between them is in conflict with the scale and character of much of the established urban landscape. There is no facile general formula for solving this dilemma; every case is a special one, and must be treated on its merits. The following are the principal factors which will be more or less relevant to each particular situation:

a) Large buildings are best related to correspondingly large open spaces, whether existing (the river, the canals, the parks) or newly created.

b) Existing methods of controlling density, plot ratio and site coverage should be reconsidered. These matters should not be treated in isolation from the three-dimensional aspects — size, bulk, height and character — of any given project.
To this end, a more definitive machinery than exists at present should be set up to enable useful prior consultation between senior planning officials on the one hand and developers and their professional advisers on the other, in the interests of speedy and satisfactory establishment of the planning authority's requirements and the avoidance of unnecessary delays or abortive work or investment on projects. Such machinery is already implicit in existing development plans, but it requires to be placed on a more formal and definite basis. Similar methods are already in operation in many European cities, Munich and Greater London being outstanding examples.

c) Agreed methods of dealing with problems of infill need to be formulated, in consultation with the architectural profession and other interests involved. This is doubly necessary in areas of high environmental quality, which are particularly sensitive. Such areas need more precise appraisal and definition than is provided by current development-plan listings.

d) The arguments for and against reproduction, replacement and reinstatement within especially sensitive areas need to be resolved, and a consistent policy formulated. These are not matters confined only to the treatment of street facades; they must be related to total building form, occupation and use.

e) There is need also for generally accepted policy on the remodelling of sound building stock which has outlasted its original functions. This refers not only to buildings of the 'classical' period but to those of the Victorian era also — perhaps even more forcefully to the latter.

f) Irrespective of the methods of design control within any particular use-zone, zone boundaries

105

should be located in back lands rather than along the centres of existing streets, save in cases where these are major traffic arteries which create their own severance. Elsewhere, care should be taken to avoid disruption — whether physical, visual or social — of established elements of the city structure. Changing use-zoning in mid-street tends to do exactly that.

5. Policy on tall buildings must be related to context as well as location

In regard to non-residential building uses, a more positive policy in regard to taller structures is recommended. 'Tallness' is a relative term, which cannot be established as an absolute figure except in the context of the building's setting, the scale of adjoining buildings, the space around or adjoining the building itself, and the presence or absence of mature trees in the vicinity. No building less than sixty feet high should be considered tall; above that figure, each case should be considered on its merits, bearing in mind the factors listed here.

Surburban district centres need the definition and sense of place which only a tall structure can provide. The television mast is a poor substitute for the historic church spire or steeple.

6. Central urban spaces must be designed in relation to adjoining buildings

Space about, between and within buildings is as vitally important an element in the urban landscape of the central city as in suburban housing areas. In the case of non-residential buildings, it is not possible to deal with this matter by way of rigid standards or rules of thumb. As stated above, the spaces about such buildings form an integral part of the design of the buildings themselves, and cannot be determined in isolation from the design process as a whole. It is recommended that the new development plans should recognise this fact, and set up the necessary machinery for prior consultation between planning officials and the intending developer and his advisers, as described at 4 b above, so that each is aware of the needs and aspirations of the other, and firm guidelines can be given to the designer at an early stage.

7. Existing trees should be preserved where practicable. New planting should be similar in scale where appropriate

The scale and character of much of the Dublin urban landscape is established by existing mature trees. It is already a major objective of the authorities to preserve all existing trees which are not demonstrably unhealthy or dangerous, and this policy should be reinforced by the making of more tree-preservation orders under existing powers, and ensuring the enforcement of those orders. In parallel with this objective should be a positive and continuing policy of new planting, with more emphasis than at present on forest hardwood species, as was the practice in former days.

In some places, trees of large growth may create engineering problems in regard to roads and services; but as with larger buildings, there are many locations where the larger species are appropriate, and full advantage should be taken of this fact as a matter of policy. Typical examples of such locations include river and canal linear parkways, parks and playing fields both new and existing, and the grounds of larger institutions, public or private.

8. Overall open space pattern and policy should be determined by Action Plans, not related to a fixed proportion for each development

The revised development plans should consolidate an extend the open space policy which is already bein implemented in newer developments on the city fring Small incidental open spaces and play areas shoul always be provided immediately adjacent to housing but it is seldom that the balance of the open spac required to serve the inhabitants (whether on per capita basis or otherwise) can best be locate separately within each individual site. (This particularly so when sites are small or irregular i shape.) Instead, Action Plans should determine i advance the size and best location for the major ope space reservation or reservations within each are; and each developer would then either reserve th necessary land or, in lieu, make a proportionate lev contribution towards the cost of providing it at th preferred location.

9. Transportation policy must be total, not piecemeal, and should respect amenity

Traffic and transportation planning must derive fron proper allocation of land uses rather than determinin them; both must be subservient to real human need, in terms of living, working and recreation. These matters have already been covered by the Dublin Transportation Study of 1971, but they need further and more detailed consideration in the light of the following principles:

a) Only an integrated transportation system which defines and respects the needs and rights of all citizens in transit — whether by public transport, private or commercial vehicle, or on foot — can be successful. Traffic intrusion is one of the most formidable of threats to the environmental quality of all parts of the urban region; in addition, it also threatens the simple working efficiency of much of the central city area today, and will continue increasingly to do so.

b) Pedestrianisation of certain areas, both central city and suburban, is inherently desirable; but in no case can it be made to work effectively unless it is intimately linked with convenient vehicle access, adequate car parking, traffic management and, above all, adequate public transport. Half measures will not do; there should be close and continuing analysis by, and co-operation between the agencies (local authority, Coras Iompair Eireann, Garda Siochana and government) jointly responsible for all traffic and transportation decisions. In particular, the public transport section needs urgent and constant re-appraisal. The total fiscal implications of providing free or heavily-subsidised public transport in certain areas should be examined impartially.

c) One possible source of revenue for such a subsidy would be to apply the proceeds (or part) of the present levy made on central city redevelopments for car parking, not towards public car parks but instead for a special central-city bus service, using smaller and more mobile vehicles at greatly increased frequency. These buses should operate on a grid system, i.e. N—S and E—W, rather than on the present predominantly radial system, inherited

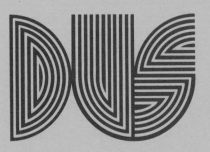

from the tramways, which is itself a major factor in central traffic concentration and congestion.

10. Central housing redevelopment should continue. Concurrently, a pilot scheme of rehabilitation should be carried out

There is a growing awareness at all levels of the need to rehabilitate or redevelop areas of central city housing, so as socially to preserve and consolidate surviving communities and to avail economically of existing and largely under-used infrastructures, both engineering and social. Further 'urban workshop' studies are needed to identify areas fit for rehabilitation: elsewhere, structures have decayed beyond redemption, and redevelopment offers the only solution.

Redevelopment densities should not normally exceed 130 persons per acre. High-rise construction is socially undesirable, its unit cost is greater, and its use saves less total land than is commonly supposed. Economic development can be achieved, even at central area densities, without normally exceeding four storeys in height.

In regard to rehabilitation, immediate action should be taken urgently by the City Authority to select and carry out a specific project in a selected area of older but still structurally-sound housing, retaining and modifying as much housing stock as possible, infilling where necessary at a similar scale, and making good deficiencies in open space and other social facilities. The project should be an experimental scheme to identify a method for further similar projects elsewhere.

11. Higher densities for housing are desirable, but high-rise dwellings are not

High-rise apartments are considered unsuitable for most families, especially those with young children, not only for social reasons, which are widely recognised, but also in terms of economics. Unit cost is higher, yet as densities are progressively increased beyond 120/130 persons per acre, the proportionate saving of land diminishes rapidly, since the amount of land needed for other related uses — roads, open space, schools and other community facilities — remains virtually unchanged per thousand of population housed. Even at densities exceeding 100 p.p.a., it is possible to house the majority of the population without exceeding four storeys in height, and in the remaining special categories anything in excess of six storeys can seldom be justified.

12. In housing, both public and private, the mix of dwelling types must be reconsidered

In housing throughout the city region, whether social or private sector, whether central redevelopment, suburban infill or completely new developments on greenfield sites, the policy should be to ensure a suitably wide range of dwellings within each locality, not only as regards variation in sizes of dwellings but also variety in the numbers of bedrooms provided within each. The exact proportion of the mix will vary from place to place; but great variety in family size and changes in social habits alike suggest the need for a range between one bed/two room dwellings at one end of the scale to five or occasionally more bedrooms plus two to three living rooms on the other to be available within a single community. Past predominance of three and four-bedroom houses has led to the twin evils of underoccupancy on the one hand and serious over-crowding on the other. This is especially true in areas of social housing.

13. Infill policy in established suburbs should be examined and intrusive uses excluded

Alike in established and in developing communities, some specific problems, new to the Irish scene but familiar from experience in other countries, are coming to the fore. These include 'intrusive' uses, such as the mammoth out-of-town public house or the sub-regional hypermarket, which rely for their service-catchment on areas much wider than the communities within which they are located or proposed. Such uses create traffic problems for the communities concerned; but their long-term effect goes farther than this, in that they threaten the profitability and thus the survival of the smaller commercial enterprises which serve only their own district. It is appreciated that present planning legislation provides no machinery for controlling intrusive uses merely on the grounds of their size, if other planning criteria can be met; but their development has already created serious socio-economic problems elsewhere, notably in Sweden and U.S.A., and extra powers are needed to control or limit their adoption here.

In established suburban communities there is also a resistance, in this case with less logic, towards changes in the pattern of residential development. These changes include attempts to broaden the social spectrum, whether by the introduction of social housing by the local authority, or the building by the private sector of apartments for sale or lease in areas hitherto confined exclusively to separate dwelling houses. In cases where such developments are desired by or acceptable to the planning authorities, consultation and education on the lines suggested at 17 are needed to allay public concern.

14. Housing sites should be selected so as to integrate with and make full use of existing landscape features

Subject only to the needs of overall good planning, as many areas as possible of existing mature landscape should be selected or reserved for residential development in Area Action Plans, and such development, whether public or private, should be designed so as to integrate housing, open spaces and existing planting. Living plant forms, unlike buildings, grow and change constantly; hence the need to ensure that the landscape elements of a development are handed over in proper condition to the planning authority, and are subsequently maintained and managed in a proper way.

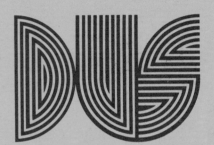

15. Full and adequate social facilities must be catered for in advance by means of agreed action plans

In newly developing outer suburbs, the provision of social and community facilities continues, as in the past, to lag behind the building of houses. In many areas, sites have not yet been allocated even for essential minima, due to absence of approved Action Plans, and existing schools, churches, shops and other community services are unable to cater for exploding population. Even where plans have been adopted, there are few cases where a full range of facilities have been built concurrently with the housing and none where they have been provided in advance, thus hindering the growth of a spirit of true community and 'sense of place' in the new settlements.

The difficulties inherent in the situation are recognised; but it is recommended that the planning authorities should strive by every means in their power to adopt at the earliest possible stage an Action Plan for each area of new development which makes adequate, realistic and agreed provision for the necessary land reservations for all relevant uses. This can only be done by active consultation with diocesan, educational and health authorities, with C.I.E. and with at least a representative selection of those private developers who will be expected ultimately to finance and build the commercial components of the development. This is already being done in areas where the city and county authorities are themselves undertaking comprehensive development; it should be extended to areas of private development as well.

The revision of the development plans is clearly of top priority for the planning authorities; but due to the absence of detailed Action Plans to clothe the skeleton of overall strategic plans, uncertainty and perhaps unnecessary disquiet are engendered in the minds of property owners, developers, the professions and the general public alike. As each Action Plan becomes available, it should be put on display, discussed with any interested parties not already consulted, and 'sold' to the public by means of lectures, exhibition, display or release to the media, as may be appropriate.

16. Existing overhead wires should be gradually replaced by underground cables

The policy of eliminating overhead wires and cables and the placing of these services underground, as is currently being implemented in new developments, should be extended also to existing areas where they still survive, as opportunity offers.

17. The Planning Authorities should take steps to encourage public participation in the planning process

In established suburban communities, the tendency to cling to existing patterns and preserve the status quo at all costs must be carefully appraised. Most such areas have in recent years set up community associations, and these vary greatly both in the size and nature of their membership and their degree of civic and social awareness. Most of these associations wield a strong influence on public opinion at all levels from local to national; most are energetic and dedicated, if not always well advised or informed. It should be the objective of the planning authorities to win over the support and co-operation of these bodies by way of encouraging their positive participation in the planning process.

At present, a great fund of energetic dedication and potential goodwill is being squandered on largely-negative attitudes. The planning authorities are well aware of the situation, and sporadic collaboration on the lines suggested is already taking place. It is recommended that planning authorities should put the education of public opinion in planning on a more formal basis.

18. Our heritage needs urgent and critical re-assessment, in order to evaluate what is worthy of true conservation, not merely great buildings and monuments, but also trees and nature, valuable man-made trivia and community structure

The recurrent theme of this entire study is the plea for conservation, in the real sense of the word, of all existing assets — not merely the more obvious assets of listed buildings or fine open spaces, but also of older but still usable housing, mature trees and planting; the incidental minutiae of canal and street furnitures; and many other small details, unimportant in themselves, which between them add up to the character and quality of our lovely, threatened city. At walking pace, the amenity and delight of that city for citizen and visitor alike, is made up not only of noble vistas of trees and buildings but also a myriad of these minor details — the quality of lamp-standards, signs, nameplates, post-boxes and other street furniture; the texture of the pavements; shop fronts and the lettering over them; railings; boundaries and small-scale planting; the colour and texture of facades as one passes them by; the occasional sculpture, civic or intimate. Where these things have style and quality, they should be conserved; elsewhere they should be replaced or created anew.

This is a call, not for blanket preservation, but for a factual critical appraisal of our assets before they are swept away in the name of comprehensive clearance and redevelopment. Moreover, assets are not confined to these mere physical objects, important though they be in giving the city its especial flavour. They include also, and most importantly of all, the living communities of the central city, and the institutions which have grown up to serve them over the years. A delicate balance must be preserved between live humanity and theoretical hygiene; and where a doubt exists, the benefit of that doubt should favour humanity.

19. Changes in statutory requirements, including by-laws and in administrative procedures and machinery, are urgently needed so that planning may be creative rather than negative, and so that architects may play a positive role in creating, preserving and restoring a better environment for the citizens of Dublin

Matters in urgent need of re-consideration include:
a) Planning blight arising from:—
   i) Road Plans ill defined, unrealistically long-term, or disruptive of existing communities;
   ii) Premature designation of obsolete or derelict, before examining their capacity for reinstatement instead of comprehensive redevelopment;
   iii) Long delays in Compulsory Purchase procedures.
b) Unrealistic zoning, with too much reliance on established uses (especially Industry and General Business) and too little regard for rational urban structure.
c) Lack of order, cohesion or central focus in new-built communities; ill-defined physical shape and structure; lack of variety in size and scale of buildings, domestic and other. Inadequate emphasis on 'village' structure within the city region.
d) Uncritical hierarchy of street widths and patterns; undue dominance of by-law thinking with regard to roads (regardless of their function); of setbacks, building lines and domestic garden sizes.
e) Neglect of railways and inadequate integration of public transport generally.
f) Absence of sufficient Action Area Plans, without which a Development Plan is only skeleton without flesh and blood.
g) **Above all, the problems of divided jurisdiction, especially with regard to the effective immunity from planning control of various statutory undertakers and others whose development is exempt. This applies with especial force to the Harbour Authority.**

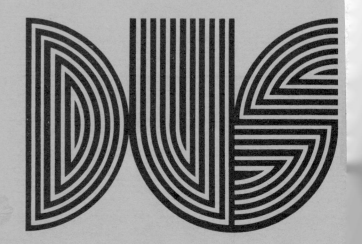